Wisdom Energy 2

Wisdom Culture

First published in 1979

Publications for Wisdom Culture
Conishead Priory,
Ulverston, Cumbria LA12 9QQ, England.

ISBN 0 86171 001 0

Designed by Robina Courtin and T. Yeshe.

Distributed in the UK and Europe by
Element Books Ltd, Tisbury, Wiltshire.

Typeset in English Times 11 on 13 point by
Red Lion Setters, London and printed and bound by
Whitstable Litho Ltd, Whitstable, Kent.

Contents

Wisdom Energy 2 was compiled and edited by Publications for Wisdom Culture.

Our warmest thanks to Geraint Rhys-Jones for his invaluable editorial advice
and assistance.

Bodhichitta p. 5
Extract from *A Meditation on Compassion*, His Holiness the fourteenth
Dalai Lama, translated and edited by B. C. Beresford, Library of Tibetan
Works and Archives, Dharamsala, 1979.

Refuge p. 7
From a teaching by Lama Yeshe at Yiga Choezin, Zurich, Switzerland, 1978.
Edited by Kathleen McDonald.

Mind impulses p. 14
From teachings by Venerable Kalu Rinpoche at his monastery, near Darjeeling,
India. Adapted by Elizabeth Harper and B. C. Beresford.

Turning the wheel p. 19   Edited by Jonathan Landaw.

Renunciation p. 26
From a teaching by Lama Yeshe at Nagarjuna Institute, Ibiza, Spain, 1978.
Edited by Thubten Wangmo.

Dissolution p. 35
From teachings by Lama Yeshe at Kopan Monastery, Kathmandu, Nepal, 1975.
Adapted by T. Yeshe.

Karma and emptiness p. 42
From a teaching by Lama Yeshe at Nagarjuna Institute, Ibiza, Spain, 1978.
Edited by Thubten Wangmo.

Reaching beyond anger p. 53   Edited by Jonathan Landaw.

Making space p. 63
From a teaching by Lama Yeshe at Kopan Monastery, Kathmandu, Nepal, 1976.
Adapted by T. Yeshe.

Mantra p. 66
In answer to a question during a teaching by Lama Yeshe at Kopan Monastery,
Kathmandu, Nepal, 1975. Edited by Chris Kolb.

Seeking the I p. 68
From teachings by Lama Zopa Rinpoche at Lawudo Monastery, Solu Khumbu,
Nepal and Istituto Lama Tzong-khapa, Pomaia, Italy, 1977. Compiled and
edited by Kathleen McDonald.

Non-duality p. 74   Edited by Chris Kolb.

Emptiness, meditation and action p. 82   *The complete path* p. 84
Poems by Kelsang Gyatso, the seventh Dalai Lama (1708-1757).
Translated by Glen Mullin.

Photographs and illustrations
B. C. Beresford: pp. 5, 9, 15, 18, 20, 36, 57, 73, 79, 82
Denis Heslop: p. 65   Jonathan Landaw: pp. 6, 13
Andy Weber: pp. 23, 25, 85, 87, 89, 91   Robert Westernberg: p. 39
T. Yeshe: pp. 21, 34, 43, 46, 50, 51, 54, 62, 70

Wisdom Energy 2

This volume is the successor to *Wisdom Energy*, a collection of talks given by Lama Thubten Yeshe and Lama Thubten Zopa Rinpoche during a tour of the United States in 1974. *Wisdom Energy 2* contains recent lectures from the United States, Europe and Asia by these and other Tibetan buddhist teachers. The unifying theme is the mahayana graduated path to enlightenment, a path of spiritual and psychological development as applicable now as it has been for the past two and a half millenia.

Dedicated to His Holiness, Tenzin Gyatso, the fourteenth Dalai Lama.
May his flawless wisdom, infinite warmth and profound skill
release all beings from the bondage of unhappiness and wrong views.

The precious awakening mind of bodhichitta, which cherishes other sentient beings more than oneself, is the pillar of the bodhisattva's practice—the path of the great vehicle.

There is no more virtuous mind than bodhichitta. There is no more powerful mind than bodhichitta. There is no more joyous mind than bodhichitta. To accomplish one's own ultimate purpose, the awakening mind is supreme. To accomplish the purpose of all other living beings there is nothing superior to bodhichitta. The awakening mind is the unsurpassable way to accumulate merit. To purify obstacles bodhichitta is supreme. For protection from interferences bodhichitta is supreme. It is the unique and all-encompassing method. Every ordinary and supra-mundane power can be attained through bodhichitta. Thus, it is absolutely precious.

Lama Thubten Yeshe

Refuge

Taking refuge is the first step on the buddhist path to inner freedom, but it is not something new. We have been taking refuge all our lives, though mainly in external things, hoping to find security and happiness. Some of us take refuge in money, some in drugs. Some take refuge in food, in mountain-climbing or in sunny beaches. Most of us seek security and satisfaction in a relationship with a man or a woman. Throughout our lives we have drifted from one situation to the next, always in the expectation of final satisfaction. Our successive involvements may sometimes offer temporary relief but, in sober truth, seeking refuge in physical possessions and transient pleasures merely deepens our confusion rather than ending it.

We should try to determine for ourselves whether or not our experiences have been beneficial. When we take refuge only in agreeable sensations or emotions, the problem of attachment is merely aggravated and we are sadly disenchanted because we expect lasting satisfaction from what turns out to be mere flickers of ephemeral pleasure. We take refuge in darkness and sink into even deeper darkness.

Buddhist refuge is a process of turning inward that begins with our discovery of our own unlimited potential as human beings. This discovery generates tremendous zeal for the development of our inborn wisdom-energy. Complete, perfect wisdom is buddhahood. Perhaps the word 'buddha' conjures up a remote and rather oriental image. But 'buddha' is just a word, and it means a totally opened mind, an 'opened lotus.' When we finally realize our human potential and arrive at this total openness of mind, we become buddhas.

However, at the outset we feel hopeless, helpless and incapable of self-improvement. Buddha seems to be somewhere in the sky, completely out of reach, and *we* are nothing. But this is not true; we should not underestimate ourselves. Shakyamuni, the historical buddha, was once even more confused than we are, but by discovering his own latent wisdom-energy he attained enlightenment. There are countless buddhas, and all living beings have the innate capacity to unify their minds with the unsurpassable clarity of enlightenment.

During Shakyamuni Buddha's lifetime, many people attained profound insight and experienced miraculous bliss as a result of merely seeing him. In spite of his bodily disappearance so long ago, we still benefit from the power of his wisdom and compassion. By cultivating our own latent powers and continuously developing our wisdom, we too can immensely benefit others. However much the world around us changes and our fortunes fluctuate, our inner world can remain stable and balanced when fortified by this profound understanding. Wisdom brings unfailing happiness, unlike those temporal objects of refuge which bring only tantalizingly brief and inconclusive moments of pleasure.

The three objects of refuge are buddha, dharma and sangha. Taking refuge in buddha involves accepting the guidance of enlightened beings as the only remedy for the confusion and dissatisfaction of our present life. This is the only way we can realize our dormant capacity for attaining inner freedom. There are two aspects of refuge: the outer and the inner. Outer refuge means seeking guidance from living buddhas, since we are unable to achieve liberation without a teacher. Buddhas also provide inspiration and are sublime models for us to emulate. When we contemplate the enlightened state, its reflection within our own mind fills us with joyful, radiant energy. This demonstrates that though at present we are not fully enlightened, the seed of buddhahood is contained within each of us. Inner refuge is directed towards this seed of enlightenment, this inner buddha-nature. We recognize that, ultimately, we are our own refuge.

If we are convinced that we are beyond hope and incapable of change, or if we think we are already perfect, then of course there is obviously no reason to take refuge. But if we honestly examine our minds, our way of life, and the pattern of our relationships we can clearly recognize our own spiritual sickness. The enlightened being we turn to at this point is in effect the doctor who diagnoses our ailments and restores us to perfect health.

The medicine prescribed by a buddha is the dharma. Dharma is wisdom: the wisdom that understands our own true nature, and reveals our own latent power of self-liberation. Taking refuge in dharma means using that wisdom *now*. This will restore our hitherto obscured sense of human dignity and make us feel that we can, after all, do something positive about ourselves. Those who take deep refuge never feel lost or desperate. Refuge frees us from such abject mental states. As our self-respect and confidence increase, our relationships with others improve. Having discovered our own inner strength we also recognize and respect the buddha-nature in others.

Dharma means understanding reality. Meditation and prayer are not dharma; they are merely tools for reaching this inner wisdom. Even if we meditate all day, but totally lacked dharma understanding, we would achieve precious little. Nor

are religious texts dharma; they are merely books about dharma, means for communicating information about dharma. True dharma or religion is a personal experience that each of us must elicit from within himself alone. There is a dharma bell within us and we should use it to awaken and activate our own dormant wisdom. Usually our mind is completely occupied with stale, unprofitable, repetitious thoughts: clutching at fantasies, and giving way to anger, jealousy or despair when they elude us. Practising dharma means ringing our inner wisdom-bell, being always on the alert and clearing away the refuse that clogs our mind, the attachments and addictions that haunt our day-dreams. By making this our daily practice, we ourselves become dharma; all our energy becomes dharma wisdom. Then we are truly taking refuge, allowing the inner dharma alone to regulate our lives.

The third object of refuge is the sangha. Sangha consists of those who are endowed with wisdom. They are like the nurses and friends who help us to recuperate from an illness. Sangha is not only those who wear red or yellow robes, but also those friends who influence us beneficiently. These spiritual friends energize and inspire us, and are therefore to be clearly distinguished from ordinary friends who hold us back. For example, everyone at this present meditation course comes from a different background and has a different outlook. But we have opened our hearts to each other and shared some profound experiences. We may in fact feel more warmly towards friends we have made here than towards older friends at home. Why is this? Because we sense a spirit of unity: together we have responded to the beauty of dharma wisdom.

True spiritual friends support one another in their practice and promote each other's growth in knowledge and awareness. We *need* support, because we are so easily influenced by our environment and by the people around us. Let us suppose that I am a heavy drinker, but have decided to take myself in hand and give the habit up. Then a friend says, 'What a hot day! Let's have a drink somewhere.' So I go with him that day, and again the next day, and soon I find myself back in the same old rut.

Moreover, in ordinary friendships we often confuse attachment with affection. For instance, my friend might show his apparent affection for me by suggesting that we go on a drinking bout together. If I decline, he might think me unfriendly and feel rejected, so I give in. This is how friends can bring us down. He didn't use threats or force but by displaying the kind of affection that consists only of clinging and attachment, he led me into a situation I would rather have avoided. It is therefore essential that we develop the wisdom-eye that distinguishes true love from mere attachment, and that can see the difference between what benefits us and what harms us. We should rely entirely on this wisdom, rather than on our ever-fluctuating emotional responses.

I can clearly see the importance of spiritual friendship when I visit my students around the world. When they are among friends in the supportive environment of a meditation course, they are happy and enthusiastic. But after they leave and try to practise on their own, their energy slowly subsides, and by the time I see them again they are back in the doldrums. This shows our need for strengthening influences that keep our energy flowing in the right channels. Whatever persons provide this influence—be they eastern or western, white or black, male or female—are of the true sangha.

It should be clear by now that the impulse to take refuge arises from seeing the necessity of developing our minds and cultivating our wisdom. Being buddhist is an inner experience, and not one that can necessarily be measured by our outward behaviour. I often meet people who hold no particular religious or philosophical views but who, in a quiet and simple way, take refuge in wisdom. They are sensitive to their own and to others' needs and try to give their lives meaning by developing themselves and helping others. In my opinion, such people are buddhists, although they may never have heard of Shakyamuni Buddha or his dharma.

Taking refuge is not difficult, but it would be a mistake to think that we can passively sit back and let buddha, dharma and sangha do the work for us. Buddha said, 'You are responsible for your own confusion, and you are responsible for your own liberation.' What saves us from confusion is our wisdom. If we take refuge while fully understanding the meaning of the three objects of refuge, our wisdom will grow and will of itself fill us with energetic determination to follow the path to liberation.

Once we have formally taken refuge, we assume a certain responsibility for our behaviour. We should watch our mind and examine the inner processes of action and reaction. 'What is my mind doing now? What impulse is arising? When I act like this, what is the result?' For example, we should observe how others react when we utter empty, unnecessary words or when we talk without understanding what we are saying. Words are very powerful. Bodily communication also has a strong effect on others; our posture, our movements and our facial expression make a deep impression on other peoples' minds. Since most of our problems involve other people, it is important to be aware of our behaviour and to avoid harming anyone.

This process of action and reaction is called karma. Karma may seem like a technical philosophical term, but it is nothing other than our own experience. It tells us what results to expect from our actions, and thus plays a vital role in spiritual practice. We want to meditate and develop wisdom, but if we make no attempt to control our behaviour and our distraught, scattered mind, we shall not get very far. For this reason we say, 'Watch your karma.' We must act with discriminating wisdom in order to create the best internal conditions for achieving our aims.

To recapitulate: buddha is the totally opened mind, the state beyond confusion; dharma is the path of wisdom leading to that state; and sangha consists of those who are endowed with wisdom and can help us along the way. It is our own life-long dissatisfaction that impels us to take refuge in buddha, dharma and sangha. We realize that clinging to daydreams and physical possessions has never given us lasting joy. Therefore, in order to rid ourselves of this dissatisfaction and gain an understanding of reality, we take refuge in wisdom: the path to inner freedom.

But you should be careful neither to exaggerate your own problems, nor to be concerned exclusively with taking refuge for yourself alone. Remember that all beings alike are confused and unhappy. Therefore, whenever you take refuge, visualize your mother and father at your side, your friends and relatives behind you, those who agitate you sitting before you, and all other beings surrounding you. With sympathy and loving-kindness think, 'All living beings in the universe, including myself, have been in confusion since time without beginning, taking refuge in fictions and constantly encountering obstacles. Now I have the opportunity to develop my human potential and become unified with the omniscience of totally opened consciousness. Instead of listening to my confused, clinging mind, I shall listen to wisdom; this is the only way to liberate myself and all beings. For this reason I now take refuge in buddha, dharma and sangha.'

Then visualize Shakyamuni Buddha before you: white light radiating from the crown of his head, red from his throat and blue from his heart. You can visualize your own spiritual teacher as this main object of refuge or, if it comes more naturally, Jesus Christ or another spiritual guide whom you revere as one who has transcended all delusion. Your object of refuge should be visualized in a gentle and loving aspect, and radiating the three coloured lights. These rays of light flow into you and all the surrounding beings, and purify all negative energy, especially despair and self-degradation.

At this point a question may arise. 'If taking refuge is a matter of relying on our own inner wisdom, why do we have a formal refuge ceremony? Why is this ritual necessary?' The answer is that it reminds us how critical the moment of taking refuge is: it marks our arrival at a crucial insight into our own nature. So many times in the past we have sought security in trivialities, but now we have discovered our innate capacity to fulfil the most exalted destiny of all: complete emancipation from suffering. We are determined that, from this moment on, rather than taking refuge in ephemeral fictions, we will take refuge in our own pure, clear wisdom-energy and set out on the path to liberation. The ceremonious action of taking refuge strengthens this determination.

Mind impulses

we practise buddhadharma to achieve buddhahood

    buddhahood means no suffering
                no defilements
                escape from cyclic existence

the seed of buddhahood is in all sentient beings
but there is a difference between
this buddha-seed
and buddhahood achieved through meditation

however, if this seed were not there from the beginning
the fruit of buddhahood could not ripen

    this is true
    and should be understood

processed milk becomes butter
purified sentient beings become buddhas
butter cannot turn into milk again
sentient beings who have reached buddhahood cannot regress

buddhahood is understanding
the emptiness of one's own mind

    no form
    no colour
    no tangibility

14

Venerable Kalu Rinpoche

these exist only in impure states
but this emptiness
        is not just void of all things
it is emptiness in which all is known
        with perfect clarity

the essence of the mind is emptiness
the nature of the mind is clarity
the mind empty and clear is buddhahood
        the state of openness

these three qualities are not separate
they are all the same

in sentient beings emptiness is not experienced
        ignorance is
clarity is not experienced
        the five senses are

the true nature of the mind is eternal
        it is unborn
        and undying
        and therefore eternal

only the body dies

ignorance
built on what our five senses receive
creates dualities
        obstructions
        and illusions

        with which we perceive the world

samsara and nirvana are not different
we only perceive them as such

there are six realms of existence
    three upper
    and three lower
in which there are many beings

the number of beings in hell
    is likened to
the number of atoms in the world,
those in the animal realm
to the number of snowflakes in a storm,
human beings to the number of stars
    in the night sky,
precious human lives to the number of stars
    in daytime

but perhaps these realms
are only states of mind

Buddha said
these states are both real and unreal
like a dream

    when you are dreaming it is real
    when you wake it is unreal
all things are real or unreal

the moon's reflection in water
    is not really the moon
but it is real
    because you can see it

in hinayana
    all illusory bad and good are stopped
in mahayana
    all illusory bad is gradually transformed
in vajrayana
    transmutation of all illusory bad to good
    is the practice

when thinking of a country
only a few places come to mind

in the same way
when thinking about the self
one can only know a small part

buddha-nature will not arise
    then vanish

mind in essence is pure

The Teaching Buddha

Turning the wheel

During the spring term of 1978, Lama Thubten Yeshe taught a course on the Buddhism of Tibet for the Religious Studies Department of the University of California at Santa Cruz. The following is an excerpt from an edition of these lectures soon to be prepared by Publications for Wisdom Culture.

The subject matter of this article is taken from a lecture in which Lama Yeshe discussed the twelve deeds of an enlightened being, specifically those of Shakyamuni Buddha (sixth century, B.C.). These are the major events in the career of all fully awakened teachers who periodically descend to renew the spiritual life of our planet.

After discussing Shakyamuni's previous attainment of enlightenment, his descent from the Joyous Pure Land (Tushita), his birth into a north Indian royal family and his early education and marriage, Lama Yeshe described how Buddha renounced his royal life of sense indulgence and adopted the spiritual discipline of extreme asceticism. Then followed an account of Buddha's dissatisfaction with this path of self-denial, his adoption of a more moderate and balanced approach to the spiritual quest, and finally, his demonstration of the attainment of enlightenment under the bodhi tree at Bodh Gaya.

This brings us to the point in Buddha's life when he was ready to begin teaching the spiritual path to others.

Shakyamuni Buddha next performed the supreme deed of an enlightened being: he began to give the teachings and spiritual instructions that release sentient beings from their suffering and dissatisfaction and lead them to the highest perfection of mind: enlightenment. This deed is commonly known as turning the wheel of dharma, and Buddha performed it in various ways for the remaining forty-five years of his life.

Although anyone who strives to reach buddhahood does so expressly to benefit others—primarily through giving teachings—Shakyamuni did not begin teaching immediately after his attainment of enlightenment. By holding back at first, he showed that the profound realizations of enlightenment are not something the ordinary, superficial human mind can be expected to grasp easily. His discovery was beyond normal conception and words, beyond expression or description. He knew how difficult it would be for others to understand what he had realized, and so he remained silent. But after seven weeks of enjoying the bliss of enlightenment in the forest by himself, he was requested to teach for the benefit of all, and agreed to do so.

Buddha's hesitation to teach until sincerely requested emphasizes an important characteristic of his teachings in general. They are never forced upon others against their will. 'Here are fantastic teachings! Why don't you come and join us?' Neither are disciples sent out into the streets to convince people how miserable they are, offering salvation to those who will come and join them. Buddha's teachings were never presented in this way, and the Tibetan traditions still follow the custom of waiting until someone asks before giving them teachings.

Why are buddhists specifically instructed not to thrust their beliefs at other people or to declare, 'I have discovered the best way of life and if you don't follow it as well, you are lost.'? According to Buddha's teachings, this approach is both unskilful and unrealistic. When someone has a profound experience, be it disastrous or fantastically blissful, it is a completely unique and personal event. It is foolish to think that an account of such a private experience will be as meaningful to another as the experience was to oneself. Even if we tell our best friend what we have discovered, it is still impossible to convey the true essence of our experience to him. Since what we are saying is necessarily expressed through words and concepts, even a very sympathetic friend will probably not grasp exactly what we want him to feel. True communication on spiritual matters is very difficult.

What this shows is that we are all living quite different lives from one another. Though we may share similar patterns of perception and behaviour, our internal experiences are unique and highly individual. We each live in the private universe of our own mind. Consequently, any attempt to force our spiritual convictions on others or share with them our devotional experiences—which, if genuine, are always of such an intensely personal nature—is misguided and can easily end in frustration and misunderstanding.

Buddha showed that there are both proper and improper times to give teachings. He always waited until he was sincerely asked before giving instruction. He knew that the very act of making a formal decision to seek help and then requesting it creates an energy within those seeking the truth that prepares them to listen intently, not merely with their ears but with their hearts as well. This is a far more effective approach than giving teachings to students who are not yet ready. In other words, the students need space. If they are not given the chance to create that space within themselves—if they are not prepared to meet the teacher halfway by opening themselves up to receiving spiritual instruction—the essence of the teachings will never penetrate their minds.

This is the enlightened being's skilful psychology. We might even call it his politics. He understands the way people think and can take the measure of their superstitious mind. He can adjust his approach spontaneously to their limitations and make sure they are ready before showing them their individual paths. His unobstructed vision embraces all existent phenomena, including the most subtle workings of our mind, and thus he can teach us accordingly.

When an enlightened being does give teachings, the strength of his realizations lends a special power to everything he says or does. Even one word of his awakened speech can satisfy the needs of many different beings. Ordinary people are limited in what they can convey with words; their speech seldom brings a sense of fulfilment. But an enlightened being's speech is different. No matter what the subject matter, each listener receives exactly what he needs.

Ordinarily, if we feel that someone is a good speaker, we might praise him by saying, 'What a powerful lecture he gave!' But from a buddhist point of view, the true power of speech is not to be found in speech itself. Behind the words, within the mind of the speaker, must be the living experience of luminous, penetrating wisdom. This wisdom gives a buddha's speech its power. Such power has nothing to do with an ordinary person's eloquence. It is solely a matter of inner realizations. Since a buddha is one whose realizations are complete, his speech has the power to affect each listener in a profound and deeply personal way. Not only that, but an enlightened being can arouse understanding without having to use any words at all.

The first formal teachings Shakyamuni Buddha gave after he attained enlightenment under the bodhi tree were given at the Deer Park in Sarnath. He delivered these teachings to the five meditators who had followed him during his six years of ascetic practices but had abandoned him when he gave up his strict discipline of self-mortification. The subject matter of this first turning of the wheel of dharma was the Four Truths of the Noble Ones. The first two truths reveal the existence of suffering and dissatisfaction in our lives and show how the source of all problems is to be found in the mind's craving attachment—whether directed towards objects of sense or perverted into extreme self-denial. The latter two truths describe the state of complete cessation of all suffering and the middle path, free of all extremes, that leads to this perfect cessation.

The second turning of the wheel began at Vultures' Peak outside Rajagriha, not far from Bodh Gaya, and dealt with the true nature of reality. These discourses on the perfection of wisdom present the profound view of emptiness (shunyata) within the context of a bodhisattva's way of life. These teachings on the lack of inherent self-existence of phenomena—their emptiness of true, substantial existence—are much more subtle than those of the first turning, and were aimed at disciples of higher intelligence and motivation.

After the first two turnings, it became necessary to clarify apparent contradictions in the teachings. While teaching the four truths, Buddha was concerned with presenting the basic path leading from suffering to liberation. Therefore he emphasized the functional nature of phenomena in those teachings. He described in detail how the mind works, how it binds us to repeated dissatisfaction and how, if properly trained, it frees us from this situation. During this first turning of the wheel Buddha spoke of the mind, or consciousness, in terms of its existence as a real entity. In the second turning, however, when he exposed the subtle misconceptions with which we view reality, he talked mainly in terms of the way in which things do *not* exist.

Buddha did not wish to confuse his followers, but he saw that the apparent contradiction between these two approaches—one emphasizing existence and the other non-existence—could cause some difficulties in the future. To avoid possible confusion he instituted the teachings of the third turning of the wheel.

When Buddha himself was presenting his teachings, even those of the very subtle second turning, he did not have to be concerned that his disciples would misunderstand what he meant. He knew the mental capacity of his audience, and was able to speak directly to each listener's heart. But he was concerned that other disciples of lesser capability and those who would come in the future might be confused. 'Why did Buddha sometimes say "yes" and sometimes "no" about the

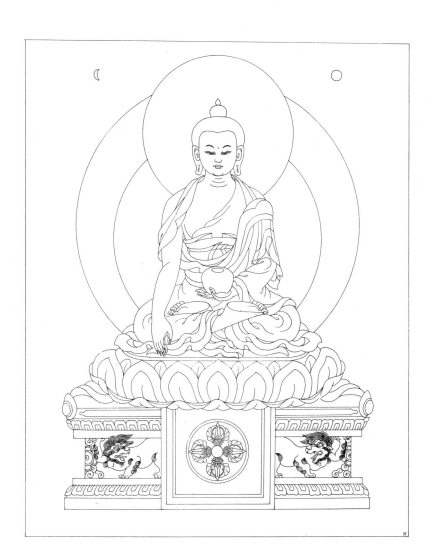

same issue?' they might wonder. For their sake, therefore, he provided further clarification.

A major characteristic of all of Buddha's teachings is that they are designed to fit the needs and aptitudes of each individual. Since we all have different interests, problems and ways of life, no one method of instruction could ever be suitable for everyone. Buddha himself explained that for the purpose of reaching a particular disciple coming from a particular background he would teach a particular doctrine. Thus there could be certain times when it might be necessary to say 'yes' and others when it would be more appropriate to say 'no,' even in response to the same question.

Because Buddhism is flexible in this way and lacks a rigid, dogmatic quality, I often feel that it is more of a psychological system than a religion. By this I do not mean that Buddhism has no religious aspect to it at all. I mean that Buddhism demands intelligent inspection of its teachings rather than blind acceptance. This emphasis on personal experience and investigation makes it unique among religious systems of thought.

If we do not take a reasoned, investigative look at the teachings, several dangers can arise. On one hand, the apparent contradictions between what Buddha taught at different times may make us question the value of his instructions altogether. With a limited vision unable to see the singleness of purpose behind this seeming discrepancy, we may find these teachings a source of confusion rather than insight. Consequently, we may disregard them entirely. On the other hand, if we adopt a very pious, unquestioning attitude towards the teachings, accepting at face value whatever Buddha said merely because he said it, sooner or later we shall suffer grievous disappointment. Someone will question our beliefs and, since they were founded on nothing but blind faith, our convictions will crumble.

According to mahayana Buddhism, there are two categories of Buddha's teachings: definitive and interpretive. Definitive teachings discuss the absolute nature of reality, while interpretive teachings deal with conventional realities and therefore must be interpreted properly before they can be understood. Because there are these two divisions, we should never feel that merely because something we read or hear is the word of Buddha we must accept it literally and without question. To adopt such an uncritical attitude towards such an important matter as spiritual development is very dangerous, and completely lacking in wisdom.

For all these reasons, in the third turning of the wheel Buddha gave guidelines for reconciling the first two turnings. He explained, for those who might otherwise have misunderstood, the way in which certain aspects of things can be

24

Vajrapani: skilful means

said to be existent and others non-existent. These guidelines show how important it is to look beyond mere words to find the true meaning of whatever Buddha taught.

Whenever Buddha spoke he stressed the importance of making a personal investigation of his words and their meaning. Only when we are convinced that the teachings are accurate and applicable to our own lives should we adopt them. If they fail to convince us, they should be put aside. He compared this process of testing the truth of his teachings with that used to determine the purity of gold. Just as we would never, without testing, pay a high price for something purporting to be real gold, we are also responsible for examining Buddha's teachings for ourselves to see whether they are reasonable and worthwhile.

Although it is traditional to divide Buddha's teachings into these three turnings of the wheel of dharma, we should not think that this is all he taught. In addition to a vast body of discourses explaining the graduated path to enlightenment, he taught the lightning path of tantra, capable of bringing a disciple to full perfection within one lifetime.

There was not a single thing Buddha did from the time he came to this earth until he passed away that was done for any purpose other than leading all living beings to deliverance from their mental and physical suffering. His formal discourses were only a part of his comprehensive teachings: the way he lived his life provided a constant example to others. And because everything he thought, said or did was born from his perfect wisdom, all his deeds were transcendental, capable of bringing ultimate peace and tranquillity to those who could take these teachings to heart.

Renunciation

Why do we human beings suffer and why are we confused? Because our minds grasp at happiness and pleasure. Failure to understand the transitory quality of temporal pleasures causes us to cling to them. But if we developed penetrative wisdom we would see that this grasping attitude only gives rise to problems. We would also understand that by overcoming our attachment to ordinary pleasure we open the way to the joy of inner liberation, liberation from suffering. Therefore we have to learn how to experience pleasure while remaining detached. In other words, we must learn about renunciation, the basic practice on the path to liberation.

Most of us do not know what renunciation means. We are disturbed when we hear about giving up attachment to sensory pleasures, which we take to mean having to suffer in order to achieve inner liberation. 'This lama is forcing me to suffer instead of making me happy.' But renunciation does *not* mean that we must give up happiness or that it is desirable to suffer. On the contrary, our aim is to achieve a state beyond suffering.

The root of all problems: difficulties in communication and relationships, neurotic fantasies, expectations, frustrations, doubts and so on, is the mind that clings to pleasure. This grasping mind is the result of our basic misconceptions about reality, and it is this grasping that causes human beings to suffer. With this mistaken approach even taking a meditation course can cause suffering. If at the beginning you expected that by the end of the course you would be blissfully enlightened, you would only be sadly disappointed.

The aim of our daily life is to satisfy each physical desire as it arises—day after day, month after month, year after year. We try to achieve happiness by perpetuating something that is essentially transitory. This expectation, stemming from a misconception, can never be fulfilled, and is therefore totally irrational. It is impossible to achieve ultimate happiness until we develop a genuine aversion to this instinctive grasping at pleasure. Unless this grasping mind is subdued, it is farcical to say, 'I am seeking inner liberation.' The methods for subduing the mind might sound simple, but they are almost completely inaccessible to most people; they find them so difficult to practise.

26

One way to understand how the grasping impulse functions is by observing how we react when we hear the names of our home town, and friends and relatives, or the sound of our own name. Strong attention and interest automatically arise in our minds. When the great yogis and saints of Tibet discovered this uncontrolled reaction in themselves they gave up their homes and families in search of ultimate tranquillity. The trouble with remaining near our home, the source of our attachments, is that we have intensely pleasurable associations with the place where we learned to smoke, drink and have marvellous parties with our friends. It is our symbol of sensory gratification and our minds cling to these memories. Even if we ourselves are not particularly attached to our friends and relatives, *they* are usually attached to *us*. The solution is relinquishment. Relinquishment is not merely physical departure but, much more to the point, inward detachment from the pleasure and involvements of home. This is renunciation.

Although many people leave their own countries for a place such as, say, Ibiza, this is not a sign of renunciation. It is their sentimental, unstable minds that make them leave home. Somehow they hope to undergo inward change by visiting a new country, but there is in fact no real difference. Their old ways of thinking and acting are the same, no matter where they are.

A great example of true renunciation is Shakyamuni Buddha. As an enlightened being he came to this earth to show others the path to enlightenment. He was born into a royal family in India and lived a life of ease, surrounded by luxury, a loving family, devoted servants and loyal subjects. But in the course of time, he came to examine the nature of that existence closely and saw only confusion and dissatisfaction in the lives of all about him. He then abandoned his kingdom to follow the life of an ascetic.

If we look beyond the mere historical facts of this story, we can understand its symbolic meaning. Buddha renounced his life of comfort and self-indulgence as a result of discovering the hidden pain inherent in every pleasure. He realized that clinging to sensory pleasure is a hindrance to inner peace, which is true happiness.

It is not surprising that we encounter powerful hindrances when trying to control our cravings for sensual fulfilment; just consider the extent to which our life is geared to chasing one pleasure after another. Attachment results from the innate belief that constant self-indulgence can satisfy the ever-present longing for happiness. But if we step back for a moment and examine with penetrative wisdom the actual nature of transitory pleasure, we shall discover a quality of painfulness inherent in that pleasure.

The painful nature of attachment is brought to light in the meditation on what are known as the eight worldly phenomena, a doctrine exhaustively expounded in Lama Tzong-khapa's text, *The Graduated Path to Enlightenment*. In this meditation we observe the unsettling effects of eight inter-related states of mind. We investigate how excited we become upon encountering the four main objects of attachment: (1) the pleasures of the six senses (the five bodily senses plus the mind), (2) possessions, (3) praise and (4) pleasant words and sounds; and how miserable we are when deprived of these four.

According to these external conditions of gain or loss we decide, 'Now I'm happy,' or 'I'm so miserable!' Deep reflection on our daily experiences with the eight worldly phenomena brings us to the conclusion that these eight attachments are incompatible with the search for inner peace. Even if we have been meditating for a long time, we cannot be called truly spiritual, truly on the path to liberation, if we still grasp at these eight worldly phenomena.

It is foolish to believe yourself spiritually motivated if you allow your mind to be driven here and there by attachment. This is like the behaviour of a monkey that spends the entire day jumping around. When you watch that monkey you think how ridiculous it is but fail to realize that you are constantly doing exactly the same thing yourself. Your own distracted mind cannot stay still for a moment, but skips from one desirable object to another. If you examine yourself you will realize that this is an accurate description of your own life, and not just one more philosophical concept. It is an objective account of the way your mind functions.

Lack of control is common to all sentient beings, from the tiniest insect right up to human beings, and is caused by ignorance. This is not to say that our own nature is essentially negative, but simply that our mind ignorantly grasps at illusory delights which inevitably disappoint us by causing suffering. Thus, for our own protection, it is essential to investigate and fully understand the real nature of our existence, and to cut through the darkness of ignorance with the sword of wisdom.

The enlightened beings' freedom from all mental and physical pain cannot be reached without renouncing attachment to sensuous pleasure. Yet we have inexhaustible appetites for good food, drinking and talking with friends, lying on the beach or hiking in the mountains. We dedicate most of our life to pleasure. It is clear we have not yet followed Buddha's advice to jettison our absurdly mistaken belief that transitory pleasures are the source of true happiness. These pleasures have no solid or enduring quality, and there is absolutely no point in pursuing them so feverishly.

No one is expected to accept these doctrines on trust. However, it is good to be open-minded and to listen to what they have to say. They show that suffering is an inward process, and is caused by our own mental attitudes. It is our responsibility to enquire into the possible truth in this. In this way we can discover for ourselves the true nature of happiness and suffering. 'Is what I am doing really making me happy or will it just let me down?' This method of contemplation is based on objective reasoning.

Another way to investigate and understand the reality of attachment is to use your past sicknesses and pains as examples. Try to remember what events led up to each of them. You will undoubtedly discover that although you looked forward to having a good time, the anticipated pleasure was eventually transformed into pain. Perhaps you went hiking and blistered your feet, or mountain-climbing and broke your leg, or went down to the beach and lay in the sun, got badly sunburnt and all your skin peeled off! Looking at these situations as a means of understanding the evolution of pain is a simple and objective way of observing the nature of transitory pleasure.

We can see that whatever we do, we do because we want to be happy. From the moment we were born until now we have looked forward expectantly to every successive pleasure and have thought, 'This is really going to be marvellous!' But confirm this for yourself. Meditate. If you use your wisdom you can see that you have been living like a butterfly fluttering in the darkness.

Sometimes we even quarrel over a few words, or our possessions, because we believe them to be the source of true happiness. It is easy to see how sick such an attitude is. Again, it stems from a misconception, an attitude of mind that attaches great importance to such trivial petty things. But the really important thing is that we should make a deliberate effort to understand how mistaken and treacherous our usual outlook is, leading as it does to nothing but disappointment and misery.

Although we may think ourselves seekers after truth, very few of us are entirely convinced of the need to destroy our misconceptions. It is as if our minds were split in half, one half determined to subjugate attachment, while the other half goes on wavering. The result is a mind like a yo-yo, constantly bobbing up and down. Half the mind wants to enjoy the beach, while the other half tries to meditate. We lack the firm, indestructible mind.

After all this talk of misconceptions and wrong attitudes, of ignorance and suffering, we might come to think our very essence impure. But it is not. A pure essence, the buddha-nature, dwells in every sentient being and is simply obscured by a veil of ignorance. Some people believe that children are naturally pure until their minds become corrupted with social attitudes. There is indeed a clear and tranquil consciousness in both children and adults, but it is obscured by misconceptions which give rise to craving and suffering instead of the joyful awareness of mind's basic purity.

At all social and cultural levels, everyone flounders in a morass of delusion. The poor think the rich happy, while the rich despise the poor, thinking them the most miserable beings. In reality, both views are wrong, since they are based on the superficial conclusion that contentment is entirely dependent on physical comforts. The opposite is in fact the case. For all beings happiness is to be found in the mind that does not pursue physical comfort.

What can we do when our deep-rooted instincts encourage us to act in ways completely opposed to our ultimate benefit? With infinite wisdom and compassion, the enlightened beings have shown us the way to deliverance from this confusion. The way is meditation on the impermanence of phenomena, and meditation on death as expounded in *The Graduated Path to Enlightenment*. By means of this meditation we can see how impermanence and death exist within us

30

from the moment of birth. With sustained meditation we shall gradually develop intuitive awareness of this truth. As we become increasingly conscious of death's approach and of its inevitability, our compulsive grasping at illusory pleasures spontaneously subsides. It slowly dawns on us that all our lives we have been working hard in the expectation of achieving comfort and peace at some time in the future. And we remember the countless beings who have lived, trapped in a maze of unfulfilled hopes and expectations, only to die in disappointment and bitterness.

Even if you are not a great yogi with indestructible meditative powers, you should at least develop the simple but clear understanding that you were not born on this earth for the sole purpose of gratifying your sense desires. This understanding can generate a power of determination to give up attachment. This determination alone becomes the cause of your future liberation from suffering. When you reach that liberated state of consciousness even a catastrophe will not affect you. Inescapable disasters happen all the time in this troubled world. Each of us therefore has the responsibility of attaining for himself a level of consciousness conferring immunity to all hardships.

Buddhism might seem exceedingly harsh in proposing a life of such extreme renunciation as to be hardly worth living. But close examination reveals a compassionate philosophy which aims to bring all beings into direct contact with their own true nature. When human beings actually follow these teachings, their innate potential for living on a higher plane is realized. Simply working for mundane comforts and necessities is the task of ants and chickens who spend most of their time seeking and consuming food and water. Our human intelligence should see beyond a life dedicated to sense gratification. At the very least we should have deeper understanding than chickens.

How was it possible for the great Tibetan yogi Milarepa to live happily alone in his Himalayan cave with no possessions, and only nettles to eat? It was possible because he had no desires. You see, suffering is not found in external objects, in a cave or in our body. It is our ignorant mind that is miserable. We can emulate Milarepa by renouncing the grasping mind as he did while at the same time continuing to lead lives free of undue hardship. We have the opportunity to do our inner work for liberation without having to struggle under harsh conditions in the mountains. The only requirement for gaining the tranquillity and contentment of Milarepa is a mind freed from attachment.

When we say liberation depends on a non-attached mind, it does not mean that you must throw all your belongings into the ocean straight after this talk. However, there are different levels of practice according to individual capacities. There are certain times when remaining in contact with the objects of attachment can give rise to great conflict. In such cases you should separate yourself physically from those objects. Generally, however, a transformation of your inward relationship with desirable objects is enough. To think that samsara consists of external objects—the world, your own body, or other people—and then to cast them away, is completely mistaken. Samsara is within you. If you do not transform your attitudes you may go away to meditate in a cave, but samsara will still be there with you.

We should avoid being over-ambitious when we first hear the buddhist teachings on wisdom, compassion and renunciation: deciding in a burst of energy to give up all our attachments and dedicate our entire lives to others. It is impossible to transform the mind instantly into that of a great ascetic. It is not as simple as going into town, buying some paint and quickly repainting the garage. It takes time to change the mind's habitual behaviour. It is only after a long, gradual process of meditating, with frequent confirmation by means of analytical wisdom, that growth and finally perfection will occur.

What can we do to get rid of attachment? One excellent practice for training the mind is to replace concern for self with concern for others. Usually we cling to our own well-being, worrying only about me, me, me. We do not allow space in our minds for others, although we may utter empty words of concern for them. This attitude can be changed first by observing how such a self-centred mind brings only harm, and then by practising a method of thought transformation in which we exchange the objects of our concern: we cherish others instead of ourselves.

Another powerful method of thought transformation is the equilibrium meditation, in which an equal feeling for all beings is cultivated. This is achieved by eliminating our usual feelings of attachment for friends and hatred for enemies through logical reasoning. By such means we can see how friends and enemies are equally kind and helpful, and thereby learn to feel only compassion and love for them, and for all others.

A third method is called giving and taking. In this meditation we dedicate all our material possessions, good qualities and merit to others, and take upon ourselves all their problems, pains and sicknesses. These sufferings are drawn into our hearts in the form of black smoke. This technique causes the ego to tremble with fear because it always wants the best for itself and tries its hardest to avoid the slightest discomfort.

Constant practice of these meditations will help to destroy this self-centred ego. These and many other thought-training meditations are found in *The Graduated Path to Enlightenment*.

Dissolution

water rushing
  down a steep mountainside,
a natural force:

there is life
  but the force
  of dying
   is there

   driving.

Many people think I am crazy when I talk to them about death.
They think I don't understand life.

   'If you think about death and suffering
   you make yourself miserable.'

They think I'm obsessed.
   'Dying is horrible.
   Why do you dwell on it?'

Ridiculous.
They do not understand life.

   we exist in a dance
   between life and death:
   a masked drama with one actor
    changing character,
   one face then another and another,
   moving
   changing.

From the first instant of life impermanence is with us.
From the moment of conception decay begins.
In the second moment of life a change has already occurred
and the first moment has disappeared. That is impermanence
                                             and death.

            'I exist.'
            'I exist' is a misconception.
            a permanent-conception.

            every energy is moving
            changing, coming and going.
            coming, then growing
            old, older and dying
            dying, dying.

When we see a dead body we never visualize our own corpse there.

            'Ah, it's dead. Horrible.
            I'm leaving now.'

We never think, 'That's me.'
There is fear. Not understanding

            that terrible corpse
            is within you now.

all sense-world phenomena
exist like a cloud.

if there is a meeting
or beginning
or contact
    there is naturally change
               separation
               and disappearance.
man and woman
friends mother father family
atoms
fire and water
things.

if there is a meeting
separation must follow
automatically. And there will be
clinging fear and suffering.

every imaginable super samsaric experience,
every contact,
every enjoyment
will disappear.
it's natural.

but we are so insecure;
we find a friend and worry
    that he will disappear.
we find pleasure and worry
    that it will end.
we are afraid to lose our home and money,
    our loved ones

    and our body.

we all fear separation
and disappearance.
this is universal fear,
but it is useless,
creating only confusion.

it is not a solution;
it is dissolution.

Recently some people went on an expedition to Mount Everest.
They were successful and reached the summit, but on the way
down one man died. They tried to revive him, but it was
impossible.

Why did they go?

Milarepa said, 'When worldly people see me they think I am
completely crazy. And, when I see worldly people I think they
are completely crazy.'

to choose coca-cola
when we could have champagne
is very stupid
isn't it.

Our materialistic lives are devoted to temporal pleasures.
We think this is the best we can do, but when death comes we
end up with nothing and we die in misery.

There is not much difference between our way of life
and a dog's life

except the potential

samsara never ends
because we don't remember death.

'Not today. No,
not today.'

life is only breath
coming in and going out.
if the breath goes out
        and does not come in again
life is finished.
that is death.

until death we are going to think,
'No. Not today.'

life is running:

death is definite
and we never know
        when it will come.

Life passes like lightning; it is there, then it disappears.
But something in us believes death will come slowly—
our permanent-conception; because we do not remember death.

wisdom-memory
        is the atomic energy
that destroys delusion,
but we forget.
we never think,
'Death is definite
and we never know
        when it will come.'

Since birth we have been collecting;
we collect friends,
we collect possessions, family, lovers, property,
this one and that one,
this and that.
We cling to each one,
and there is fear.
And when we die
not one of these things helps.
Instead of helping, our collection destroys us.
Because we did not remember death.

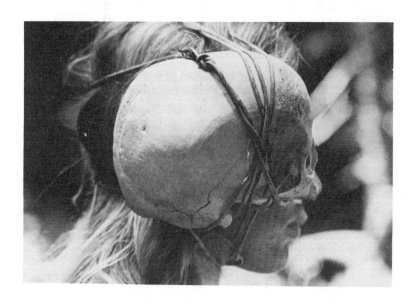

it will come,
definitely.

and the time
      is never certain.

'Ah, today I'm alive.
I'm all right.
Not today.'

why not?

'Your father died today.'

O.K. It was time for him to die.
Everybody has to die.
Now that he is dead, it's my turn.

     Do you understand?

I must do something right now.

     Like this: if I know that within ten days someone is going
to cut off my nose, but I don't know who and I don't know when, I'm going to be
so careful; I'll protect my nose as much as possible and not waste time putting on
make-up to make it beautiful.

     We have this choice:

to die is a natural thing,
but it is possible to die
joyfully

like going home

Karma and emptiness

You are all interested in dharma and meditation. But what is dharma, and how do we meditate? Basically, dharma is anything that causes our delusions, our disturbing thoughts, to subside; it is anything that brings us peace of mind and liberation from confusion and suffering.

Buddhadharma teaches methods to purify the mind of negativities and to develop our human potential to the fullest. Some of these methods, such as not harming others, generating compassion and practising generosity, are shared by other philosophical and religious traditions. Other methods are uniquely buddhist. Two of these, karma and emptiness, are the heart of dharma. Karma is the law of cause and effect, and emptiness is the ultimate nature of reality, devoid of all misconceptions.

Let us begin with karma. Every single action performed by body, speech or mind eventually produces a specific reaction. For example, an unwholesome attitude will definitely culminate in problems and suffering, while a wholesome, clean, clear mind always brings happiness. We have all noticed that when our mind is full of confusion everything we say comes out in a confused way. This illustrates the evolutionary link existing between all actions and their consequences. Although this link seems obvious when analysed, it is not always apparent. When we catch ourselves saying something senseless or nasty we are apt to say, 'Oh, I don't know why I said that; it just came out that way.' To assume that there is no particular reason for our uncontrolled actions is a mistake. Not one word has ever been uttered that was not motivated by either a positive or negative attitude.

Understanding the karmic connection between causes and effects will give us the energy to change ourselves. Nevertheless, it is essential to approach our practice with patience and wisdom. Changing our habitual behaviour is not easy. It is not like making instant coffee; it takes time. Change occurs gradually because the various negative attitudes and delusions have different degrees of strength. Therefore each mental problem must be treated according to its particular nature, be it extremely subtle and deeply embedded in our consciousness, or quite evident and within reach. The logical approach is to concentrate first on purifying gross negativities before attempting to root out the deeper subtle ones.

42

The important point is that removing the more obvious faults is something we can do *now*. It is much wiser to work in an area where success is possible rather than to reach for the impossible.

For example, when washing a dirty rag it is impossible to remove the stains and odours from it immediately. The initial washing takes care of the first layer of dirt but only after it is washed and wrung out two or three times are all the stains finally removed. The root delusions—attachment, anger and ignorance—are the stains polluting our mind and, of these, ignorance of reality is the most deeply ingrained and the most difficult to remove. Cleansing the mind is an evolutionary process and the only way to ensure positive change is to work on the gross delusions now and tackle the more subtle ones later.

Throughout your dharma practice you must never push yourself, but on the contrary you should try to be at ease and to do only what is possible at the moment. If you push yourself beyond your capacity you may shock your entire nervous system, thus producing an extremely negative reaction; you may even give up trying to deal with your delusions altogether.

Even though we are adults we have the minds of children. A child's mind requires especially tender care; we need great skill and patience to deal with it. It cannot endure being squeezed, or pushed beyond its limits. Yet many spiritual seekers are perfectionists whose egos impel them to try and advance too quickly. They are severe and ruthless towards themselves, and end up in a state of tension. They become frustrated and angry with themselves and everyone around them. Of course it is good to strive for perfection, but we must be practical. It is best to go by degrees, step by step. Otherwise you are likely to jump in too quickly and break your leg. To succeed in your dharma practice it is best to be at ease, relaxed and down-to-earth, to adjust the intensity of your practice day by day according to your situation.

Being practical includes being open to adapting your practice to external conditions. For instance in this meditation hall we are sitting together cross-legged on oriental rugs, surrounded by beautiful statues and paintings of the buddhas; incense smoke fills the air and candles burn on the altar. Naturally it is easy to meditate in such a positive atmosphere.

However, if you find yourself in another environment, such as in a train or on a 'plane, this does not give you an excuse for abandoning your practice. Just because there are no visible images of the buddhas you feel that Buddha is not there. The whole place seems to lack spirituality and you feel as if you are drowning in samsara. Or perhaps at home your family will not allow you to have an altar, or images of the enlightened beings visibly displayed. And because you know how much it would upset them you refrain from saying your prayers out aloud. Then thinking back nostalgically to that peaceful meditation hall, you think, 'Now it seems as though I'm in a different world. No pictures of the spiritual teachers or buddhas, no candles or incense, and I can't chant my prayers. How can I possibly practise dharma?'

Such dissatisfied thoughts are examples of the dualistic mind at work. You have managed to rationalize your way out of doing your meditations, not realizing that the beauty of the graduated path to enlightenment is that it explains how to meditate in any environment—whether eating, drinking, talking, travelling or whatever. Religious paraphernalia are useful of course, but not absolutely essential to the practice. By the way, I find the bathroom an excellent place to have a quiet, undisturbed meditation away from noise and confusion. It is a good place for taking refuge.

Actually it is possible to find a dharma teaching in everything we see—television, films, newspapers, the wind blowing, the movements of the ocean or the changing of the seasons. If we observe the world from the dharma viewpoint we can gain a profound understanding of reality, including impermanence and the law of cause and effect. 'All these things are changing, just as I am.' We usually walk about in a dream, unaware of the changes and movements going on around us. Either that, or we take them for granted. It is easy to dismiss what television and movies are trying to show as mere fantasies. Such prejudices only increase our ignorance and close the door to wisdom. If, on the other hand, we open our wisdom eye and let the universe reveal its reality, we can increase our knowledge and practise dharma any time and anywhere.

By allowing everything we see to remind us that the law of cause and effect governs all change, that each transformation has a definite reason, we shall gradually understand karma. We will stop assuming that our experiences come to us readymade, like instant coffee. Sensitivity to our nervous system's constant state of flux will become more acute as we watch how our mind and body change again and again.

Once a deep understanding of cause and effect arises within us, and we see that every single action has a definite consequence, we shall realize how important it is to be conscientious about everything we do. Awareness of karma brings spontaneous awareness of our own behaviour. By realizing that positive actions lead inevitably to happiness and negative actions to suffering, we become more discriminating and more conscious of the nature of our own activity. If the law of cause and effect does not guide our life, however, there is no dharma practice, and without such practice only ignorance and suffering remain.

Sustained conscious awareness of our physical, verbal and mental actions from the moment of waking to the moment of falling asleep at night is more profound and penetrating than one hour's meditation every morning. This makes sense; an hour's meditation is nothing compared to a day's practice. And if we consider the enormous benefits of even one day's awareness of karma we can guard against the apathy and depression that often infect our practice.

45

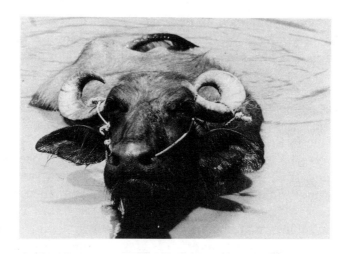

One reason for stressing the value of watching our karma is that westerners are always so interested in meditation. They love meditation, but they are not so happy when they are offered teachings on karma. They complain that karma is too heavy. But we must not give way to anxiety. Our body, speech and mind are *already* heavy; it does not take the teachings to make them heavy; we *are* heavy.

I am not implying that meditation is unimportant, but even if we have trouble doing formal meditation, we can still practise dharma perfectly well. Meditation then means always being watchful of our actions and cultivating an attitude of loving-kindness rather than one of exploitation. This is meditation. In fact, in view of our present level of spiritual development, this sort of approach to our practice can be even more precise and realistic than meditation on profound tantric subjects.

If we can awaken to the immediate moment we have achieved something important. Take the present moment. We are all physically here in this room, but our minds are somewhere else, most likely thinking about the future. 'After this meditation course I'll ... .' We are dreaming about something else while the present moment is slipping by. Even as I am talking to you my mind is thinking of Tibet. I am not really with you.

There is a powerful dharma method for bringing the mind into the present. Each morning, as soon as you wake up, you should think in this way: 'How fortunate I am to be still alive, and a human being rather than a dog or a chicken.

With this human body and mind I have the power to understand my mind and to practise dharma. This is something that animals cannot possibly do. So I dedicate this day to the attainment of enlightenment. In order to reach that goal quickly I must avoid impure actions, and emanate a positive vibration towards others.' The power of this dedication will help to keep your awareness and control at peak level throughout the whole day.

Many people spend their time thinking about what they want to do tomorrow, in twenty-five years, or for the rest of their lives. This is foolish. The events that will happen in twenty-five years' time are nothing but the result of a process of transformation going on from moment to moment—even *now*. The present moment evolves into the following one, which changes into the next one. Today changes into tomorrow, tomorrow into next week, next year and so on. If the process of evolution did *not* depend on events taking place at this very moment, there would be nothing happening twenty-five years from now.

Although the future depends on the present, it is the human ego's nature to worry about the future instead of how to act *now*. When you meditate, meditate. When you eat, eat. When you cook, cook. Try to replace your fantasies about the future with awareness of the present moment. Only then are you being realistic. It is ridiculous to be overly concerned with what is going to happen in the future, since your projections about it are merely a product of your own hallucinating mind. Unfortunately, however, it is a common pastime to make concrete plans for the future. 'I must be sure to have enough of this and plenty of that for the next few years.' Perhaps you will die before the week is out. Worrying about the future is simply a waste of time and energy.

There are many people who do not believe in enlightenment because they have never met or seen an enlightened being. I would ask them, 'Can you see tomorrow?' If not, where do all the concrete conceptions that form the basis for all their future plans come from? They worry about what will happen in a future they cannot see, yet they do not accept enlightenment on the grounds that they cannot perceive it.

From the karmic viewpoint we *should* be concerned about the future, but our present concern is wrongly associated. The general confusion in relation to the future comes out in the kinds of questions often posed to lamas and priests: 'When I die will I go to heaven or hell?' 'Do you think I'll be happy next year?' With dharma wisdom bringing to mind the law of cause and effect, it is easy to predict what the future will bring. A positive, wholesome attitude today bodes well for tomorrow. If the mind-stream is clean and clear today, then it is certain to be clean and clear tomorrow. So we *do* have the ability to predict the future: by using our own wisdom. We can see that living and dying happily or miserably depends on maintaining a positive or negative attitude from now on. It is needless to run to our spiritual teachers to ask them what is going to happen. We have the choice between dying the miserable death of a cow or experiencing the blissful death of a meditator. It depends on our karma. If the causes and conditions—milk, heat and so on—come together in the evening, the result will be a bowlful of yoghurt next morning.

It is silly to ask exalted beings and clairvoyants if there is going to be a worldwide disaster during the next few years. Disasters are happening all the time. By understanding karma we can see that as this solar system is the product of delusion, it is naturally besieged by wars and catastrophes. Therefore it is waste of energy to fret and worry about it. What we *should* worry about is keeping ourselves as peaceful, positive and aware as possible. That is all we can do.

Let us now turn to the other essential aspect of the dharma, that of analyzing the ego. The ego is the mind that misunderstands the nature of the I, the self. We generally feel that the I exists somewhere vaguely within the body but our ordinary superficial mind never attempts to pinpoint it precisely. To gain a correct picture of reality, it is necessary to investigate deeply and try to find out exactly where this I resides. Otherwise we shall continue to be deluded, fooled by a view that, although superficial in some ways, still clings to a deep and concrete sense of self. When we make a thorough search for our self, looking throughout our entire body and nervous system, we can never find it. Sometimes we may think we have located it, but upon closer examination we can see that we have been deceived.

Although there is a specific technique for trying to locate the I, each one of us must approach our investigation in terms of the highly individual and instinctive way we habitually refer to ourselves. Some people have a vague sense that the I is in their chest; others feel it is in their head or stomach. When someone is troubled and holds his head between his hands, or slaps his forehead or clutches at his heart, this indicates where he most strongly feels his I at that moment. Each of these gestures is a symptom of the person's ego projecting a particular sense of self. My symptom, for instance, is to hide behind my monk's robes. The fact that we each have our own set of symptoms shows that the intuitive feeling of I is merely an interpretation of the ego. If the I were something substantial, there would be much more agreement as to what and where it is.

The self imagined by the ego has a mysterious, inaccessible nature. This is because there is no general agreement about its qualities or location; we each have our own feelings about it. This is precisely why each person must seek his imagined I *himself*. No one can do it for him. Yet even with the most precise introspective wisdom, seeking the I in every cell of the body, it remains impossible to locate. It is like a thief who sneaks up on us when we are not looking and hides when we turn around. When we are relaxed and not on guard, he advances on tip-toe like a demon ready to attack but if we chase him he suddenly disappears as if swallowed up by the earth. This is exactly how our devious mind deceives us. The ego's hallucination of a concrete, self-existent I is like the thief. We are certain it is there but as soon as we look for it, it disappears.

Our mind will go on cheating us until we finally catch it in the act! Meanwhile we shall continue to carry around a strong intuitive feeling of I, and a vague notion that it exists somewhere, probably in the body. The only way to arrest this fantasy is to observe the object of our hallucination, in this case our own self; examine it carefully and see what it *really* is. As the imagined I is like a sneak-thief, it is necessary to use a special trick in order to capture it. We must somehow bring the object in question into clear view for close inspection. Because the imagined I comes up most strongly in highly emotional states, we should take advantage of those situations, look at the obvious feeling of I that has arisen, and try to locate and identify it. Another effective technique is deliberately to evoke during meditation an emotional crisis in order to bring this feeling of I to the surface. In either case, the meditator must be extremely alert if he is to capture this image before it disappears. Through this practice he will eventually discover that the self he has always believed to exist has no basis at all. It was, and is, nothing more than a fantasy.

All our suffering and fears exist only because of our passive acceptance of the ego-projected illusory self. Because this self appears to exist concretely, it seems to be deeply involved in experiences of gain and loss and the accompanying feelings of depression and elation. This is, in fact, the basis of all our suffering.

At some point in his contemplations the practitioner clearly realizes that all his misery springs from an image projected by his own distorting mind, an image that has no basis in reality. At this point he has reached an indestructible state of mind, beyond all fear. When Tibetan meditators reached this level of realization they used a skilful technique for putting their new experience to the test. They imagined themselves involved in an extremely frightening or emotional situation and then watched their reactions. If no great sense of I fearing loss or pain arose in their minds, they could be certain of their inner achievements. This sort of experimentation is similar to the way ideas are tested in scientific studies. Here, however, the experiment is internal and very personal.

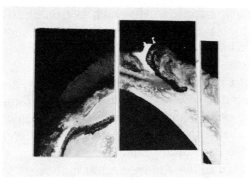 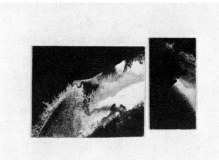

According to the philosophy of the great Indian teacher, Nagarjuna, the self that appears intuitively to our minds does not exist anywhere within the entire atomic structure of the body. This view is not to be confused with nihilism which asserts that nothing exists at all. What, then, *does* exist? The answer lies in Nagarjuna's philosophy of the middle way which denies the existence of the self fantasized by the ego, while asserting that of the dependently arising, relative self.

This is not simply some philosophical concept; I am not interested here in talking about philosophy. This is a practical method for discovering what is real and what is not. And if you look into this for yourselves you will see how your own ego imagines the existence of something that does not exist at all.

When a baby is born, the parents arbitrarily give a name to the little bubble that has suddenly appeared. They have no logical reason for choosing that specific name for that particular bubble. 'Do you like the name Christina?' 'Yes, I like it.' 'Good, then let's call her Christina.' It is not as if the mother and father can see that the baby's innermost self or consciousness belongs, by its very own nature, to a category that is always called 'Christina.' Or that something within that baby is just waiting to be called by its *real* name, 'Christina.' In light of Nagarjuna's philosophy, it is just a matter of a bubble appearing and then being called by a name. The combination of word and bubble is Christina.

But the ego is not satisfied with being just a bubble with a name. Therefore it confuses the issue by imagining that something else exists. 'I am more than just a

bubble; I have my own existence apart from that.' The nature of the ego is to be dissatisfied, and it cleverly improves and beautifies its identity by fashioning it into shapes and colours of its own imagination. Just as it is never satisfied with any amount of wealth or beauty, neither is it happy with being merely a name and a bubble. It cannot accept simple reality: the way things actually are. For instance, now that I am in Spain I no longer like being Tibetan. I would rather be a handsome Spaniard with a nice moustache. Wherever I go I want to be something different. I cannot admit or accept who or what I am. It is incredible how unrealistic the ego is! Its world is like plastic: pure imitation.

In reference to the ego's fantasy world, Buddha said, 'All is illusion.' To understand the true meaning of this statement, let us first see what is meant by the ego's world. Your world is all that you see, hear, smell, taste, feel and think; in other words it is made up of all your sense perceptions. Each person's ego creates its own personal world. You are not living in my world; you are living in your own ego's illusory world. Yet when some people hear that all is illusion they misinterpret it to mean that nothing matters. 'Fantastic! I can steal, drink, take drugs and hallucinate on LSD to my heart's content. Who cares? It's only an illusion anyway.'

There are various terms used in referring to the ultimate nature of reality. Sometimes it is called emptiness, since the true nature of all phenomena is empty, as opposed to the ego's imagination, which is full. Full of what? Full of concepts, expectations, anxieties and projections that have nothing to do with reality. Ultimately, all things are empty. Reality is also called voidness, voidness being the opposite of the solid, concrete world imagined by the ego. All phenomena, both samsaric and spiritual, are void by their very nature.

It is essential to eliminate the ego's basic misconception about reality, because this is the root of all suffering. The ego's view is debased and unrealistic, and produces a low opinion of oneself and of others. It underestimates our true potentialities and qualities, thereby creating a feeling of insecurity and defensiveness. Furthermore, with this sort of negative attitude we easily get involved in arguments and fights with one another. The ego is political by nature. If there were no ego, there would be no reason to quarrel.

The ego's misconceptions about reality also keeps us in bondage, whether it be the iron bondage of worldly existence or the golden bondage of a spiritual way of life. The iron bondage is our continual mental and physical suffering in the cycle of dissatisfied existence known as samsara, while the golden bondage is that of being enslaved to misconceptions and false philosophies.

Many philosophies have a good appearance, an attractive golden facade. However, no matter how respectable they might seem, these incorrect views still bind us to ignorance and suffering. The highest goal is to be free of *all* bondage. But I do not mean being free in the revolutionary sense. Maybe you think that this lama is trying to start another Spanish revolution! No, I am just trying to provoke a revolution in your minds.

52

Reaching beyond anger

The following article was compiled from discourses given by Geshe Kelsang Gyatso at Manjushri Institute, England in 1978 when he was lecturing on Shantideva's famous text A Guide to the Bodhisattva's Way of Life (Bodhisatt-vacaryavatara). *The full commentary to this work will be brought out by Publications for Wisdom Culture under the title* Meaningful to Behold, *and the present article will form part of the sixth chapter dealing with the practice of patience. A translation of Shantideva's root text, prepared by Stephen Batchelor in accordance with an oral teaching of Geshe Ngawang Dargyey, will soon be published in Dharamsala, India by the Library of Tibetan Works and Archives.*

In his *Guide to the Bodhisattva's Way of Life*, the great Indian master Shantideva declared that there is no greater evil than anger. It is a force capable not only of negating the effects of whatever positive actions we have done in the past, but also of preventing us from attaining goals we have set for ourselves, whether they be achieving full enlightenment or merely improving our mind. The antidote to anger is patience, and if we are seriously interested in advancing along the path of spiritual development, there is no greater practice than this.

The value and importance of developing patience become obvious if we look at the visible faults of anger. When we are overcome by hatred, we immediately lose all peace of mind and even our body becomes uncomfortable. We are plagued by restlessness, the food we eat seems unpalateable and we find it nearly impossible to fall asleep—and whatever sleep we do manage to get is fitful. Anger transforms even a normally attractive person into an ugly, red-faced demon. We grow more and more miserable and, no matter how hard we try, we cannot control our feelings.

One of the most harmful effects of anger is that it robs us of our reason and good sense. Wishing to retaliate against those who have harmed us, we expose ourselves to great personal danger merely to exact our petty revenge. We lose all freedom of choice, driven here and there by an uncontrollable rage. Sometimes this blind rage is even directed at our loved ones and benefactors. In a fit of anger, forgetting the immeasurable kindness we have received from our friends, family and teachers, we might strike out against and even kill the ones we hold most dear. It is no wonder that a person habitually controlled by anger is soon avoided by all who know him. This unfortunate victim of his own hostility is the despair of those who formerly loved him, and eventually finds himself abandoned by everyone.

It is generally assumed that anger arises in response to meeting someone we do not like, but in truth the situation is often the exact opposite of this. It is the anger already within us that transforms the person we meet into our imagined foe. Someone who is anger-prone lives within a vision of paranoia surrounded by enemies of his own creation. The false belief that everyone hates him can become so overwhelming that he might even go insane, the victim of his own delusions.

It is very important to recognize the true cause for whatever unhappiness we feel. If we are forever blaming our difficulties on others, this is a sign that there are still many problems and faults within our mind. Why is this? If we were truly peaceful inside and had our mind under control, nothing that happened would be able to disturb that peace and no one we met would ever appear to be our enemy.

To one who has subdued his mind and eradicated the last trace of anger, all beings are like friends. A bodhisattva, for instance, whose sole motivation is the welfare of others, has no enemies. Very few people wish to harm someone who is a friend of all the world. And even if someone did harm or abuse this high-minded being, the bodhisattva could remain at peace. With his mind dwelling in patience, he would remain calm and untroubled, able to smile at his assailant and even treat him with respect. Such is the power of a well controlled mind. Therefore, if we sincerely want to be rid of all enemies, the wisest course of action is to uproot and destroy our own anger.

We should not think that this is an impossible task or an unreasonable goal. Skilled doctors are now able to cure illnesses that were fatal only a short time ago and have eradicated other diseases completely. Just as scientists and physicians fought and finally overcame these diseases, so can we eradicate the disease of anger infecting our mind. Methods to gain release from this crippling delusion are available to all of us. They have proved their effectiveness whenever people have sincerely put them into practice, and there is no reason why they cannot work for us as well. Imagine what the world would be like if we all conquered our anger! The danger of a third world war would evaporate; armies would become unnecessary and soldiers would have to look elsewhere for work. Machine guns, tanks and atomic bombs—instruments useful only to the angry mind—could be put away as all conflicts, from wars between nations to quarrels between individuals, came to an end. And even if this universal harmony is too much to hope for, imagine the freedom and peace of mind each of us individually would enjoy if we exorcised this hateful demon within us.

What are the methods for overcoming and finally destroying our anger? There are two allied approaches for accomplishing this aim. The first, which has already been mentioned, is to gain as clear a recognition as possible of the many faults and disadvantages of anger. We need to identify this poisonous delusion, and not any external force, as our true enemy. This recognition is necessary if we are to channel our efforts in the right direction. The second approach is to gain a deep understanding of *why* we become angry and then work to counteract and eliminate the causes we have uncovered.

The root cause of anger, as with all the other delusions, is our innate ego-grasping: the ignorant view that holds onto the self and all other phenomena as inherently self-existent. If we cut through this ignorance there will no longer be any basis left for unhappiness or dissatisfaction. Yet ego-grasping is a deeply entrenched habit of mind, and it requires a great deal of time and effort to gain the profound realisations required to uproot it completely. However, there are other more immediate causes for the arisal of anger, and since these can be dealt with right away, it is worthwhile to concentrate on them in the beginning of our practice.

Anger is a response to feelings of unhappiness, which in turn arise whenever we meet with unpleasant circumstances. If we are prevented from fulfilling our wishes or forced to deal with a situation we do not like—in short, whenever we have to put up with something we would rather avoid—our uncontrolled mind immediately feels unhappy. This uncomfortable feeling eventually turns into anger, and we become even more disturbed than before. For example, a boy who wants very much to be with his girlfriend will become extremely resentful of anyone or anything that prevents him from doing so. If she refuses to see him or leaves him for someone else, his unhappiness can easily turn into rage. Therefore, aside from innate ego-grasping, frustration of our desires is the main reason for anger to arise.

To overcome anger we have to learn new ways to respond to frustration. Since it is unreasonable to expect that we can fulfill *all* our desires, we must cultivate a more realistic and balanced approach to the problems of life. The methods for training our mind in this more realistic approach are included within the practice of patience. The more clearly we understand that the sole function of anger is to make us miserable, the more motivated we shall be to train ourselves in patience.

In general there are three spheres of activity involved in the practice of patience: (1) learning how to endure suffering with acceptance and joy, (2) thinking about our spiritual training and (3) refraining from retaliation. At first glance these practices may seem a bit strange and even unnatural, but if cultivated with the proper understanding they can liberate our mind from one of its most obsessive delusions and confer great peace and joy. It is therefore worthwhile to

56

Geshe Kelsang Gyatso

persevere in these practices even though they may seem unusual in the beginning.

Concerning the first practice of patience, learning how to deal with and to accept inevitable suffering, we should remember that wherever we find ourselves within cyclic existence (samsara) only a few circumstances bring happiness, while the causes of misery are plentiful. This is the very nature of samsara: its sufferings are infinite while its joys are small. And all the suffering we encounter is the result of actions we ourselves have done in the past. Since this is the case, we should learn to endure what is unavoidable rather than fight against the inevitable.

If we learn the proper way of enduring the unpleasant, unhappy thoughts will never arise to bother us. We can avoid the many hindrances, including anger, that disturb both our everyday life and our practice of dharma. But if we are impatient with our suffering we shall only make ourselves more miserable. For example, perhaps our body is attacked by a disease. If we have a method for enduring and accepting the pain—for instance, by seeing it as a means of exhausting negative karma—we may discover that the pain actually subsides. However, if we refuse to deal realistically with the discomfort, cursing our illness or letting ourselves become depressed, then not only might our physical pain increase but we shall experience the additional suffering of mental torment as well. Our anger has only made matters worse, creating the cause for further suffering in the future.

There are many benefits of meditating on the patient acceptance of suffering. In addition to maintaining a calm and peaceful mind in the face of distressing circumstances, we shall be able to gain a clear and dispassionate view of just how unsatisfactory our samsaric existence really is. There is a certain mental stability to be had merely from recognizing that every experience of pain or discomfort is the fault of our being caught up in samsara—the fault of being born, living and dying in a state of unknowing and confusion. This recognition, which cannot dawn on a mind consumed with anger, is the basis for developing renunciation: the spontaneous and continuous wish to attain complete and utter freedom from every trace of dissatisfaction in life. Without firm renunciation there is no way to reach any of the higher goals along the spiritual path, and thus no way to experience the boundless happiness of liberation and enlightenment. If this precious mind of renunciation can be generated through our practice of patient endurance, then it is certainly worthwhile to put up with whatever discomfort we may have to experience, and to do so joyfully.

We should not be discouraged by the difficulties involved in practising patience. Shantideva mentions the ancient Indian people of Karnapa who endured the tremendous hardships of combat and self-mortification merely to propitiate a certain deity. Nowadays as well there are many famous examples of athletes—prizefighters, weight-lifters, football players and others—who inflict extraordinary physical punishment upon themselves in the pursuit of their professions. It is easy to think of many other people who voluntarily endure great suffering merely to earn some money or enhance their reputation. If for limited goals they can bear such tremendous difficulties, why can't we accept the difficulties and inconvenience involved in our pursuit of complete human perfection? Why should we be so easily discouraged by discomfort?

The second form of patience is directly involved with our spiritual training, our study of dharma. When circumstances arise that might easily provoke anger, we should refrain from giving in to our habitual patterns of reaction; instead we should remember to turn to the teachings of dharma for a solution to our problems. It requires patient mindfulness to keep the dharma uppermost in our thoughts at the very moment we are experiencing difficulties, but the more adept we become at summoning our wisdom, the easier it will be to transform even the most unsatisfactory situation into an opportunity for real spiritual growth.

Certain aspects of dharma training are quite difficult and great patience is needed merely to study them. For instance, we already mentioned that ego-grasping is the root cause for all of our delusions and suffering. The antidote to this grasping mind is the profound view of emptiness (shunyata) which understands directly that all things are empty of self-existence and arise instead in dependence upon circumstances, causes and our conceptualizations. Because of our beginningless conditioning in ignorance, this view is not at all easy to understand. However, once we become familiar with it through a process of systematic study, contemplation and deep meditation, our understanding will become a powerful ally and a great protection for our mind. We shall see that all causes and effects lack inherent existence and are therefore like an apparition. If we can remember to look at things in this light when difficulties present themselves, our anger and indeed all our delusions will vanish.

Thirdly there is the patience of not retaliating when harmed. Difficulties involved in this particular practice can be overcome if we combine with it a method for generating compassion. For example, if someone harms us we should not only think, 'He is hurting me only because he is deluded' but also, 'He is hurting himself, too.' If we remember what people do while controlled by greed, jealousy, anger and so forth, we can begin to imagine the tremendous suffering these poor, deluded people are heaping upon themselves. When we think of the immediate and future harm their delusions will inflict upon them, we shall better understand why they often harm us as well. If we contemplate this deeply, not only shall we overcome the wish to retaliate, but we shall also be able to generate great compassion for those who would disturb our peace.

Under the influence of anger a person who normally cherishes himself more than anything else in the world is even capable of committing suicide. If the force of his delusions can drive him to such desperate measures, then we can certainly see how it can cause him to inflict pain on others. Anger can so totally rob a person of his freedom of action that it is unreasonable for us to feel hostility for anyone under its sway. If we cannot generate compassion for such an unfortunate person, at the very least we should be able to refrain from getting angry at him.

The ability to practise the patience of non-retaliation requires a great deal of prior mental preparation. Without such preparation it is unreasonable to expect that we can remain unruffled when someone interferes with us. If we have trained our mind well beforehand, however, we shall find that we can avoid getting angry—or the need to suppress our anger—even in situations of great provocation.

Let us imagine that someone is about to attack us. He picks up a stick and hits us with it. Shouldn't we get angry at him? After all, he has harmed us. At this point someone might argue, 'Don't get angry at the man; get angry at the stick. After all it was the stick that was the immediate cause of your pain.'

Such an argument is hardly convincing. We would certainly retort, 'The stick didn't hit me by itself. Without the man who wielded it, it would have had no power to hurt me. It's the man himself I should be angry with.'

If this is the line of reasoning that keeps us from getting angry at the stick, we should apply it to the man as well. We should realize that he was manipulated by the power of his anger in exactly the same way that the stick was manipulated by the power of his hand. With scarcely any control over his mind, he was at the mercy of his delusions. Therefore, if being harmed is going to provoke anger in us at all, we should direct our wrath against the actual cause of our pain: the delusion of anger itself.

(It should be noted that we are concerned here with our own internal, mental reaction to experiences of pain and discomfort. No suggestion is being made that we should passively let ourselves be beaten up or harmed merely for the sake of practising patience. If there is a way open for us to prevent this man from hurting both us and himself, then certainly we should stop him. The question here, however, is: What should we do with our mind once the harm has been received? The entire practice of patience, and indeed of dharma as a whole, is to provide protection for the mind because ultimately it is our mind which determines whether we are happy or miserable.)

Another powerful method for overcoming anger and refraining from retaliation is to see all undesirable situations as a reflection of our own faults and shortcomings. If we are the object of someone's abuse, for instance, we can remember the teachings on cause and effect and think, 'I wouldn't be suffering this harm now if I hadn't abused someone similarly in the past.' The same approach can be used in regards to sickness, injury or any other problem. Our ability to use this way of thinking effectively depends upon our acquaintance with the karmic laws of cause and effect. Once our understanding of and conviction in this law becomes firm—once we realize that we always reap the fruit of our own actions, receiving good for good and evil for evil—we shall be able to remain inwardly peaceful and calm even in the most adverse circumstances. We can view the harm we receive with a sense of relief, seeing our pain as the repayment of a long-standing debt. This is certainly preferable to becoming angry and upset, which only incurs the future debt of more pain and anguish.

Despite what has been said, there still may be great doubts in our mind about this practice of patience. 'If I don't retaliate when others harm me, what will people think of me? What will happen to my reputation?' To answer this doubt we have to examine the value of fame, reputation, praise and the like. How do these benefit us? Will others' opinions help us develop our minds, ensure our long life or prevent us from becoming sick? Since they can do none of these things, why should we be unhappy when our praises are left unsung or our reputation suffers?

If our only interest is obtaining the transient pleasures of a good reputation, wealth and sense gratification, then there is no fault in behaving in the same heedless way we have always done, to the neglect of our spiritual training. But anyone who desires ultimate happiness and has even an inkling of how far the mind can be developed will never be satisfied with such insubstantial pursuits. A good reputation, wealth and a respected position in society are, it is true, generally quite beneficial. Like all experiences of pleasure they are the result of our own skilful and virtuous actions of the past. Yet if our attachment to these fortunate conditions forces us to become angry when they are threatened, they will cease to be beneficial and will become instead only the cause of more suffering. We should understand that it is not external circumstances that make us happy, but the way our mind relates to them. The development of patience and the elimination of anger improve the way our mind functions and increase our happiness. This is why such spiritual practices are recommended.

Those who become elated when praised or miserable and angry when criticized were referred to by Buddha as 'the childish ones.' Children at the beach love to make sand castles. When the surf eventually sweeps away these piles of sand, they weep with disappointment, 'My castle is gone!' Similarly, if we allow our mind to be swept here and there by the changing waves of praise and criticism, we are as foolish as these children. On the other hand, if we can train ourselves in such practices as patience, compassion and generosity, it is possible to achieve true emotional and spiritual maturity. Since there is no better way to make use of this precious human life, we should be willing to follow these practices even though they entail difficulty.

May these precious teachings of the great bodhisattva Shantideva be of benefit to those who wish to follow them.

Making space

Bodhichitta is the essential, universal truth.

This most pure thought is the wish and the will to bring all sentient beings to the realization of their highest potential, enlightenment.

The bodhisattva sees the crystal nature that exists in each of us, and by recognizing the beauty of our human potential, always has respect.

For the disrespectful mind human beings are like grass, something to be used. 'Ah, he means nothing to me. Human beings are nothing to me.'

We all try to take advantage of someone else, to profit only for ourselves. The entire world is built on attachment. Big countries overwhelm small countries, big children take candy from small children, husbands take advantage of their wives. I make friends with someone because he can benefit me. It is the same with the rest of the world. Boyfriends, girlfriends. Everybody wants something.

The desire to make friends only for the other person's benefit is extremely rare; however, it is very worthwhile. Buddha explained that even one moment's thought of this mind dedicated to enlightenment for the sake of others can destroy a hundred thousand lifetimes' negative karma.

We have attachment which makes us tight and uncomfortable. But even a tiny spark of bodhichitta's heat makes the heart warm and relaxed.

Bodhichitta is the powerful solution, the atomic energy that destroys the kingdom of attachment.

Bodhichitta is not emotional love. By understanding the relative nature of sentient beings and seeing their highest destination, and by developing the willingness to bring *all* beings to that state of enlightenment, the mind is filled with love born from wisdom, not emotion.

Bodhichitta is not partial. Wherever you go with bodhichitta if you meet people, rich people or poor people, black or white, you are comfortable and you can communicate.

We have a fixed idea; life is this way or that. 'This is good. This is bad.' We do not understand the different aspects of the human condition. But, having this incredible universal thought our narrow mind vanishes automatically. It is so simple; you have space and life becomes easier.

For example, someone looks at us, at our home, at our garden and we freak out. We are so insecure and tight in our hearts. Arrogant. 'Don't look at me.' But with bodhichitta there is space. When someone looks we can say, 'Hmm. She's looking. But that's O.K.' Do you understand? Rather than feeling upset you know it is alright.

Bodhichitta is the intoxicant that numbs us against pain and fills us with bliss.

Bodhichitta is the alchemy that transforms every action into benefit for others.

Bodhichitta is the cloud that carries the rain of positive energy to nourish growing things.

Bodhichitta is not doctrine. It is a state of mind. This inner experience is completely individual. So how can we *see* who is a bodhisattva and who is not? How can we *see* the self-cherishing mind?

If we feel insecure ourselves we will project that negative feeling onto others.

We need the pure innermost thought of bodhichitta; wherever we go that will take care of us.

Mantra

It is a common misconception that reciting mantras is an external and unnatural mental exercise, rather than an internal and spontaneous occurrence. Reciting a mantra, however, does not mean the mere vocal repetition of speech syllables. Many meditators know from experience that the act of reciting mantras transcends external sounds and words. It is more like listening to a subtle inner sound that has always inhabited our nervous system.

When we receive the transmission of a mantra from a qualified teacher, the integration of that mantra's wisdom into our consciousness is greatly facilitated. Through the wisdom-power of mantra we can easily communicate with our own true inner wisdom, while remaining free of external distractions. The normal world-oriented state of mind prevents us from letting go of emotional problems as they arise. These distractions invade our mind and constantly impede our concentration. When we recite a mantra this mental agitation spontaneously subsides, leaving our mind at peace. Mantra brings about a stronger, more integrated, single-pointed concentration. It quickly rids us of interruptions caused by our habitual sensory response to external stimuli.

When trying to develop penetrative insight into emptiness, it would be absurd if we had plenty of time for eating and sleeping but no time for reciting mantras. Normally, we have plenty of time for listening to meaningless gossip but no time to develop our wisdom by listening to our inner sound. In actual truth, our inner sound can be the means of attaining perfect samadhi, perfect absorption into reality.

The existence of inner sound cannot be denied. Our nervous system has its own specific inner sound. This is not something that mahayanists have invented; it is an objective reality that exists within us. For example, the sound 'ah' exists within us from the moment of birth. All speech sounds are derived from 'ah'. Without 'ah' there could be no other sound.

Mantra becomes more powerful when imparted by a qualified teacher who has deep inner experience of the mantra. He has acquired the mantra's power from his own teacher, and has gained further experience while in retreat. Furthermore, a good teacher creates a situation that heightens our receptivity to the wisdom transmitted by the mantra.

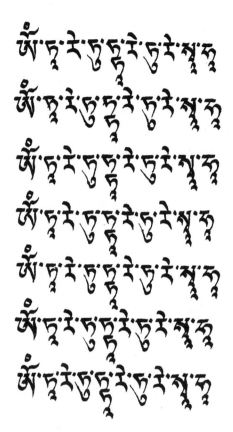

Om tare tuttare ture soha
the mantra of Arya Tara

The mantra functions in many ways. The reciting of a mantra a given number of times, combined with concentration, opens our mind instinctively to super-normal powers and insights. Mantras can also be used as therapy for the sick, and can bring peace to the mentally disturbed. This has been the experience of many meditators.

Mantra is energy. It is always pure, and cannot be contaminated by negative thought processes. As mantra is not gross energy, it cannot be corrupted the way sensory phenomena are corrupted by our own minds. One can easily discover the power of mantra for oneself by embarking upon a meditational retreat.

Those endowed with skilful wisdom will naturally attain realizations through the power of mantra. Practitioners of mantra yoga will discover that their inner sound becomes completely one with the mantra itself. Then even their normal speech becomes mantra.

Seeking the I

All the problems we encounter in samsara: the cycle of repeated death and rebirth, have their source in the ignorance that grasps at things as though they were self-existent. Our situation in this cycle is similar to being trapped in a large building with many rooms and doors, but with only one door leading out. We wander hopelessly from one part of the building to another, looking for the right door. The door that leads us out of samsara is the wisdom that realizes the emptiness of self-existence. This wisdom is the direct remedy for the ignorance which is both cause and effect of clinging to self, and which believes the self or 'I' to be inherently and independently existent. In other words, the I appears to be something it is not: a concrete, unchanging entity, existing in its own right, and our ignorant mind clings to this mistaken view. We then become addicted to this phantom I and treasure it as if it were a most precious possession. Wisdom recognizes that such an autonomously existing I is totally non existent and thus, by wisdom, ignorance is destroyed. It is said in the buddhist scriptures that to realize the correct view of emptiness, even for a moment, shakes the foundations of samsara, just as an earthquake shakes the foundations of a building.

Each of us has this instinctive conviction of a concrete, independently existing I. When we wake up in the morning we think, 'I have to make breakfast,' or, 'I have to go to work.' Thence arises the powerful intuition of an I which exists in its own right, and we cling to this mistaken belief. If someone says, 'You're stupid,' or 'You're intelligent,' this I leaps forth from the depths of our mind, burning with anger or swollen with pride. This strong sense of self has been with us from birth—we did not learn it from our parents or teachers. It appears most vividly in times of strong emotion: when we are mistreated, abused or under the influence of attachment or pride. If we experience an earthquake or if our car or 'plane nearly crashes, a terrified I invades us, making us oblivious to everything else. A strong sense of I also arises whenever our name is called. But this apparently solid, autonomous I is not authentic. It does not exist at all.

This does not mean that we do not exist, for there *is* a valid, conventionally existent I. This is the self that experiences happiness and suffering, that works, studies, eats, sleeps, meditates and becomes enlightened. This I does exist, but the other I is a mere hallucination. In our ignorance, however, we confuse the false I with the conventional I and are unable to tell them apart.

This brings us to a problem that often arises in meditation on emptiness. Some meditators think, 'My body is not the I, my mind is not the I, therefore I don't exist,' or, 'Since I cannot find my I, I must be getting close to the realization of emptiness.' Meditation which leads to such conclusions is incorrect, because it disregards the conventional self. The meditator fails to recognize and properly identify the false I that is to be repudiated and instead repudiates the conventional or relative I that *does* exist. If this error is not corrected it could develop into the nihilistic view that nothing exists at all, and could lead to further confusion and suffering rather than to liberation.

What is the difference, then, between the false I and the conventional I? The false I is merely a mistaken idea we have about the self: namely, that it is something concrete, independent and existing in its own right. The I which does exist is dependent: it arises in dependence on body and mind, the components of our being. This body-mind combination is the basis to which conceptual thinking ascribes a name. In the case of a candle, the wax and wick are the basis to which the name 'candle' is ascribed. Thus a candle is dependent upon its components and its name. There is no candle apart from these. In the same way, there is no I independent of body, mind and name.

Whenever the sense of I arises, as in 'I am hungry,' self-grasping ignorance believes this I to be concrete and inherently existent. But if we analyze this I, we shall find that it is made up of the body—specifically our empty stomach—and the mind that identifies itself with the sensation of emptiness. There is no inherently existing hungry I apart from these interdependent elements.

If the I *were* independent, then it would be able to function autonomously. For example, my I could remain seated here reading while my body goes into town. My I could be happy while my mind is depressed. But this is impossible; therefore the I cannot be independent. When my body is sitting, my I is sitting. When my body goes into town, my I goes into town. When my mind is depressed, my I is depressed. According to our physical activity or our state of mind, we say, 'I am working,' 'I am eating,' 'I am thinking,' 'I am happy,' and so on. The I depends on what the body and mind do; it is postulated on that basis alone. There is nothing else. There are no other grounds for such a postulation.

The dependence of the I should be clear from these simple examples. Understanding dependence is the principal means of realizing emptiness, or the non-independent existence of the I. All things are dependent. For example, the term 'body' is applied to the body's components: skin, blood, bones, organs and so on. These parts are dependent on yet smaller parts: cells, atoms and sub-atomic particles.

The mind is also dependent. We imagine it to be something real and self-existent, and react strongly if we hear, 'You have a good mind' or, 'You're terribly confused.' Mind is a formless phenomenon that perceives objects, and is clear in nature. On the basis of that function we impute the label 'mind.' There is no functioning mind apart from these factors. Mind depends upon its components: momentary thoughts, perceptions and feelings. Just as the I, the body, and the mind depend upon their components and labels, so do all phenomena arise dependently.

These points can best be understood by means of a simple meditation designed to reveal how the I comes into apparent existence. Begin with a breathing meditation to relax and calm the mind. Then, with the alertness of a spy, slowly and carefully become aware of the I. Who or what is thinking, feeling and meditating? How does it seem to come into existence? How does it appear to you? Is your I a creation of your mind, or is it something existing concretely and independently, in its own right?

Once you have identified the I, try to locate it. Where is it? Is it in your head ... in your eyes ... in your heart ... in your hands ... in your stomach ... in your feet? Carefully consider each part of your body, including the organs, blood vessels and nerves. Can you find the I? If not, it may be very small and subtle, so consider the cells, the atoms and the parts of the atoms.

After considering the entire body, again ask yourself how your I manifests its apparent existence. Does it still appear to be vivid and concrete? Is your body the I or not?

Perhaps you think that your mind is the I. The mind consists of thoughts which constantly change, in rapid alternation. Which thought is the I? Is it a loving thought ... an angry thought ... a serious thought ... a silly thought? Can you find the I in your mind?

If your I cannot be found in the body or the mind, is there any other place to look for it? Could the I exist somewhere else or in some other manner? Examine every possibility.

Once again examine the way in which the I appears to you. Has there been any change? Do you still believe it to be real and existing in its own right? If such a self-existent I still appears, think, 'This is the false I which does not exist. There is no I independent of body and mind.'

Then mentally disintegrate your body. Imagine all the atoms of your body separating and floating apart. Billions and billions of minute particles scatter through space. Imagine that you can actually see this. Disintegrate your mind as well, and let every thought float away.

Now, where are you? Is the self-existent I still there, or can you understand how the I is dependent, merely attributed to the body and the mind?

Sometimes a meditator will have the experience of losing the I altogether. He cannot find the self and feels as if his body has vanished. There is nothing to hold on to. For intelligent beings this experience is one of great joy, like finding a marvellous treasure. Those with little understanding, however, are terrified, or feel that a treasure has just been lost. If this happens, there is no need to fear that the conventional I has disappeared—it is merely a sensation arising from a glimpse of the false I's unreality.

With practice, this meditation will bring about a gradual dissolution of our rigid concept of the I and of all phenomena. We shall no longer be so heavily influenced by ignorance. Our very perceptions will change and everything will appear in a new and fresh light.

Closely examine the objects, such as forms, that appear to your six consciousnesses, analyzing the way in which they appear to you. Thus the bare mode of the existence of things will arise brilliantly before you.

These lines from *The Great Seal of Voidness*, a text on mahamudra by the first Panchen Lama, contain the key to all meditation on emptiness. The most important factor in realizing emptiness is correct recognition of what is to be discarded. In the objects appearing to our six consciousnesses there is an existent factor and a non-existent factor. This false, non-existent factor is to be discarded. The realization of emptiness is difficult as long as we do not recognize *what* the objects of the senses lack, i.e., what they are empty of. This is the key that unlocks the vast treasure house of emptiness.

But this recognition is difficult to achieve and requires a foundation of skilful practice. According to Lama Tzong-khapa, there are three things to concentrate on in order to prepare our minds for the realization of emptiness: first, dissolution of obstacles and accumulation of merit; second, devotion to the spiritual teacher; and third, study of subjects such as the graduated path to enlightenment and mahamudra. Understanding will come quickly if we follow this advice. Our receptivity to realizations depends primarily on faith in the teacher. Without this, we may try to meditate but find we are unable to concentrate, or we may hear explanations of the dharma but find that the words have little effect.

This explanation accords with the experience of realized beings. I myself have no experience of meditation. I constantly forget emptiness, but I try to practise a little dharma sometimes. If you also practise, you can discover for yourselves the validity of this teaching.

Lama Thubten Zopa Rinpoche

Non-duality

During the summer of 1977, Lama Yeshe visited Madison, Wisconsin and stayed at the home and centre of his teacher, Geshe Lhundup Sopa. While there he gave six weeks of teachings on Maitreya's Discriminating between Relative and Ultimate Reality (Dharma-dharmata-vibhanga-karika) *from which the following is a brief extract. Maitreya's root text is a dynamic, meditative approach to the profound view of reality, emphasizing the non-dual nature of all existence. In the following selection, Lama Yeshe comments on some central ideas from this text and offers an introduction to non-dualistic thought.*

There is no purpose or value in studying this subject merely for intellectual stimulation. That would be a complete waste of time. The knowledge contained in Maitreya's teaching is incredibly deep but only worthwhile if pursued with the proper motivation. Unless we engage in this study for the purpose of eradicating our psychological problems we would probably do better to spend our time trying to make coca-cola; at least then we could quench our thirst.

We have all probably heard a lot of gossip about mahamudra meditation. 'Maha' means great and 'mudra' means seal. If I have a government seal no one impedes or harasses me. When I have an official government seal on my passport I am free to go wherever I choose. The seal of mahamudra is similar, but here we are talking about a state of mind that is beyond our ordinary dualistic view of existence. This is the great seal that sets us free from the prison of samsara. Mahamudra itself is non-duality. It is the absolute true nature of all universal phenomena, be they internal or external.

What is meant by the term 'non-duality'? All existing phenomena, whether deemed good or bad, are by nature beyond duality, beyond our false discriminations. Nothing that exists does so outside of non-duality. In other words, every existing energy is born within non-duality, functions within non-duality, and finally disappears into the nature of non-duality. We are born on this earth, live our lives and pass away all within the space of non-duality. This is the simple and natural truth, not some philosophy fabricated by Maitreya Buddha. We are talking about objective facts and the fundamental nature of reality, neither more nor less.

74

Maitreya

If we are to achieve the realization of mahamudra it is essential to develop skill in the art of meditation. But to meditate properly we must first listen carefully to a faultless exposition of the subject matter. This will give us an accurate and precise understanding of the aim of meditation. If we have a clear intention of putting such explanations into practice in meditation, then merely to hear the teachings becomes a powerful experience instead of some kind of superficial intellectual 'trip'.

To understand that the dualistic mind, lost in false discriminations, is the source of beginningless and endless suffering for oneself and others is to have a truly valuable insight that will profoundly change the quality of our daily lives.

The dualistic mind is, by nature, contradictory. It sets up an internal dialogue that has forever disturbed our peace. We are always thinking, 'Maybe this, maybe that, maybe something else'—and so on. Dualistic thinking perpetuates a conflict within our mind. It causes us to be agitated and deeply confused. When we know that this confusion is the result of a mind conditioned by the dualistic view of reality, we can do something about it. Until then it will be impossible for us to come to grips with the problem because we have not correctly identified its true cause. It is not enough merely to treat symptoms. It is clear that we must completely eradicate the source of problems if we are to become truly problem-free.

As our understanding and knowledge of mahamudra deepens we shall come to realize that the way things appear to us is simply a projection of our mind. For example, it is not a question of whether Madison, Wisconsin exists or not, but whether the *way* in which we perceive Madison exists in reality or not. It should be clear that this is not the same as the nihilistic assertion that nothing exists. We are simply seeking the correct view of reality.

To clarify this point further we can investigate the fantasies we project upon our friends and the people we live with or meet every day. Our dualistic mind superimposes an attractive or repellent mask upon the presented image of everyone we meet, with the result that reactions of desire and aversion arise which colour our attitudes and our behavior towards this person. We begin to discriminate: 'He is good' or 'She is bad.' Such rigid, preconceived attitudes make it impossible to communicate properly with even our close friends, much less with the profound wisdom of an enlightened being, or buddha.

If we persistently investigate the inner workings of the mind, we shall eventually be able to break through our habitual overconcretized mode of perceiving the universe and let some space and light into our consciousness. In time we shall have an insight as to what non-duality actually is. At that time we should simply meditate without intellect or discursive thought. With strong determination we should merely let the mind meditate single-pointedly on the vision of non-duality, beyond subject/object, good/bad, and so on. The vision of non-duality can be so vivid and powerful that we feel we can almost reach out and touch it. It is very important simply to mingle the mind with this new experience of joy and luminosity without seeking it by analysis. We must realize directly that non-duality is the universal truth of reality.

In directing our mind along the path of dharma it is best not to expect too much too quickly. The path is a gradual process to be negotiated step by step. Before one can follow practices that bring a quick and profound result there are preparatory practices that must be done. Lama Tzong-khapa, for example, strove very hard for the realization of shunyata, or emptiness, but met with no success, in spite of being a renowned teacher with many disciples. Finally Manjushri, the embodiment of perfect wisdom, revealed to him that he must make a retreat in order to purify his mind-stream completely of all gross and subtle delusions, as well as their imprints. Tzong-khapa then withdrew to a cave, where he did three and a half million prostrations as well as innumerable mandala offerings and other preliminary purification practices. As his thought-stream became purified, his understanding of emptiness began to deepen. This transformation continued until he finally achieved full awakening.

It is helpful if we understand that the realization of non-duality has many levels or degrees. From the philosophical point of view there are two Indian schools of mahayana buddhist thought: the Chittamatrin or Mind Only school and the Madhyamika or Middle Way school with its Prasangika or Consequentialist subdivision. Both of these schools agree that the dualistic view is deceptive and therefore not ultimately true, and both assert that non-duality is the absolute nature of all things and *is* ultimately true. Though the Mind Only and Consequentialist schools agree on these points, their understanding of what is meant by non-duality varies somewhat.

From the Consequentialist point of view the Mind Only doctrine presents a helpful approach to conventional truth but does not accurately describe the absolute true nature of reality. In other words, they state that the Mind Only view of reality is still tainted by superstitious beliefs. Despite this, even the Consequentialists agree that if we are able to realize the Mind Only view we are qualified to practise the profound methods of tantric yoga and reach unimaginably high levels of understanding.

What we should know is that the Mind Only school contends that all objects of the sense world are simply manifestations of mental energy and do not exist externally at all. According to the Consequentialists it is more correct to say that the existence of all things *depends* upon recognition by an imputing consciousness. Both schools attach great importance to the mind's role in determining the way in which entities arise, but the higher Consequentialist school says that to assert that there are no external phenomena whatsoever—that there is nothing other than mind—is an error. Such a view deviates from the true middle path that transcends all extremes.

The Mind Only meditators destroy the dualistic view by seeing that all objects in the field of the six senses are no more than mere projections of our mind itself. All relative phenomena arise and disappear like the bubbles in a glass of coca-cola. In this analogy, coca-cola corresponds to the mind itself while the bubbles arising within it are all relative phenomena perceived by the six senses. Can the bubbles in coca-cola be separated from the coca-cola? No. Therefore, as they are not separate, they are non-dualistic. When a deep understanding of this pervades our consciousness, the foundations of samsara are shaken.

The Consequentialists transcend dualism by realizing that both subject: mind, *and* object: the sense field, are illusory and empty of self-existence. Subject and object are mutually interdependent: they cannot exist independently of one another. For this reason the Consequentialists do not agree with the Mind Only position that mind itself—as the source and substance out of which all relative phenomena arise—has true, inherent self-existence. According to the Consequentialists, all phenomena, including mind, are empty of even the slightest trace of self-existence.

The fully awakened Lama Tzong-khapa, in his work *The Heart of Perfection*, explained that first we must master the Mind Only view because from that elevated position we can easily progress to the highest, most sublime view, that of the Consequentialists. It is for this very reason that Maitreya Buddha explained the Mind Only doctrine. It is the bridge we rely upon to cross over from a completely materialistic outlook to the transcendental view of reality which is beyond all extremes.

When I expound subjects of this kind, I try to avoid being too philosophical—dwelling on 'Mind Only says this,' 'Consequentialists assert that'—especially when we are dealing with such subtle and penetrating texts as this one. Generally speaking, this teaching by Maitreya Buddha is considered to be a Mind Only text; however, it is not necessarily confined to a Mind Only interpretation. This entire text also lends itself perfectly to a Consequentialist explanation of reality and the two levels of truth. It is essential to know these two levels of truth well because

when we successfully reconcile them we arrive at a true understanding of things *as they actually are*, and become free of all suffering and its cause.

I would like to go over this point once more. Each phenomenon has two characteristic qualities or natures. One is its relative appearance, its colour, shape, quality, texture, and so forth. This is termed 'deceptive truth' because it appears to exist independently of causes and conditions. In terms of this level of truth we discriminate subject and object, this and that, and so on. Even though all phenomena, internal and external, partake of this relative nature, they nevertheless arise, exist and pass away without ever departing from the sphere of non-duality. The second level of truth is the non-dualistic, absolute, true nature of things, which spontaneously co-exists with all phenomena.

Phenomena themselves and the absolute nature of phenomena, have distinctive qualities; they are not the same thing. All phenomena simultaneously possess a relative or conventional mode of existence as well as an absolute, true nature, which is non-dualistic. Certain energies come together and produce a relative phenomenon. Its relative mode of existence is dualistic, and appears in terms of a subject and object relationship; yet all things arise within the space of non-duality.

Relative phenomena (dharma) are like bubbles. They are the dualistic vision of the dualistic mind. Therefore they are not truly existent or real. Absolute, true nature (dharmata) is non-dualistic. It is, therefore, real or true. Though relative phenomena and the dualistic vision do exist and function, they are not ultimately true. That is the point.

When we say that all relative phenomena have the nature of non-duality we are not saying that all existence is emptiness or absolute truth. All relative existence is *not* absolute truth. Relative phenomena are not absolute phenomena. But every existing energy, whether relative or absolute, has the characteristic nature of non-duality.

I want to explain this further. When we contemplate non-duality the dualistic vision should disappear. Therefore we can say that non-duality is absolute nature. But can we say that *all* non-duality is absolute nature? No. Why not? Because, although all phenomena partake of the nature of non-duality, we do not have to perceive non-duality itself in order to perceive conventional reality. My head, for example, has the nature of non-duality, and yet we cannot say my head *is* absolute truth or emptiness. In order to apprehend my head you do not need to apprehend non-duality. Yet a doubt may persist: 'If my head has the characteristic nature of non-duality why then, when you apprehend my head, do you not apprehend non-duality itself?' Because there is the veil of dualistic mind between you and my head.

It may become clearer with another example. Which is the more pervasive, the population of the United States, or the population of Madison, Wisconsin? The population of the United States includes the population of Madison, but the inhabitants of Madison do not pervade the population of the entire United States. Non-duality is like the population of the United States, and all relative phenomena are like the inhabitants of Madison. All relative phenomena are embraced by non-duality, because they arise within the space of non-duality; all relative phenomena demonstrate non-duality.

To conclude, in order to understand non-duality we have to understand emptiness. We can say therefore that non-duality is emptiness. But all the bubbles of relative phenomena, though they themselves are ultimately non-dual, are not emptiness. Relative and absolute truth do not pervade each other, but both are pervaded by non-duality. If we can understand the distinctive characteristics as well as the non-contradictory natures of these two levels of truth, we can gain freedom from even the subtlest delusions of mind. There can be no stronger motive for study and meditation than this.

80

Kelsang Gyatso, the seventh Dalai Lama

Emptiness
meditation
and action

An image of a sun enthroned
   in the heavens,
Radiating one thousand beams
   of light:
     Were one to shower bright rays
     of love upon all beings,
How excellent.

An image of a kingly eagle
     gliding high in space:
Were one's mind to glide
     without grasping
In the space of truth itself
     clear and void,
How excellent.

An image of a grey wind flowing
    forcefully through the sky:
Were one to maintain an energy flow
    always beneficial to others,
The best of spiritual practices,
    never artificial,
How excellent.

An image of fresh, white clouds,
Bright, pure and drifting
    freely:
Were one to build clear,
    blissful meditation
    in the perfect mystic mandala,
How excellent.

An image of the vast sky everywhere
    free of obstruction:
Were this song on emptiness,
    meditation and action
Without hindrance to benefit the world,
How excellent.

The colophon: During one retreat, His Holiness the Seventh Dalai Lama arose from a morning meditation session and saw a pair of eagles flying south, playing freely between fluffy white clouds sharply defined against a dazzlingly bright sky. He was moved to compose the above song.

The complete path

Homage to the all-kind spiritual guide
Who is inseparable from the Bodhisattva of Wisdom,
And who is the primordial Buddha Vajradhara
Performing the dance of a human.

The spiritual guide, all powers unified,
At one taste with the beyond-samsara nature
        of all Buddhas of the ten directions,
Cannot be known by the intellect
Nor described in petty words.

For those of us born into this degenerate age,
He is kinder than all the Buddhas;
For, like pushing gold into a beggar's hand,
He shows us the richness of the Sutras and Tantras
        and points to the path free of extremes.

A teacher of such great kindness
Should be approached with profound appreciation:
Look unflinchingly for the face of the true
        teacher
Who understands fully the ultimate nature of mind.

Manjushri
buddha of wisdom

Whatever you want for yourself and others
With a human form is easily attained;
Disengage yourself from meaningless efforts,
Strive to accomplish the highest of goals.

Because all things composite are impermanent,
Life changes and never abides;
That change is the basis of all suffering,
For the samsaric mind fills with frustration
      on watching its creations continually fade.

This body formed from sperm and ovum
      emits foul odours from every hole.
It is not a thing to cherish;
Yet, due to the power of delusion,
We have become its servant.

Not to mention months or years,
We cannot be sure it will endure even until
      tomorrow.
If one is weak and facing death,
So what if the tree of wealth and friends is laden?

The higher you climb in samsara, the higher
    the cliff on which you perch;
The more things you own, the tighter
    you are bound.
The dearer you hold someone, the greater
    the chance he will hurt you;
The faster you subdue enemies, the faster
    their numbers increase.

This body is a thing borrowed for a moment,
And possessions are things stored for others.
Now we dally with them,
But quickly are they lost and, misused, end
    only as sources of misery.

Therefore no worldly position
Is worth the effort of gaining.
Turn your back on that which only handicaps:
An unburdened mind is joy supreme.

The pinnacle of aims is to follow this path:
Body, speech and mind kept stainless with pure
    self-discipline,
Mind held in samadhi blissful and clear, and
Wisdom seeing all realities of every situation.

*Chenrezig
buddha of compassion*

The mother beings wandering in the six realms,
To me, their son, are pieces of my heart.
For many times have they soothed my troubles
And in infinite ways have they brought me joy.

These infinite beings, so kind, are covered
    by the fog of ignorance.
Constantly slashed by the whips of delusion,
They have no chance to lay down
The burden of misery from their minds.

Therefore whenever you meet anyone,
Greet him with eyes smiling with love.
Why mention that you should not even consider
Holding evil intentions or deceptive thoughts?

Aspire to practise purely and selflessly,
Not being discouraged even for a moment.
Exerting yourself in the Bodhisattva ways
Just as does a warrior of the ten stages.

The way people and things seem to be
        other than projected labels
Is a distortion created by deluded mind.
If we look at the root of things,
Emptiness is clearly understood.

And in the vast space of perception of emptiness,
Mental grasping for ultimates subsides.
Then one looks into the face of the world,
Everything is seen as being without essence.

Understanding interdependence we understand emptiness,
Understanding emptiness we understand interdependence;
This is the view which is the middle,
And which is beyond the terrifying cliffs of
        eternalism, nihilism, neither and both.

The tantric master, he one with Vajradhara,
Must then stamp your mind with the four initiations,
Introducing you to the blissful path of the
        three kayas
And to the ultimate nature of body and mind.

*Dorje Sempa and
Dorje Nyema Karmo*

Thus can one bathe consciousness in the innate clear light,
Shape energies into the form of a tantric deity,
And abide unwaveringly in the deep, clear yoga
Which does not divide meditation from non-meditation.

All things that appear in the world are
Seen as an inconceivable abode of wisdom,
And the endless beings dwelling therein
Are known to be but an ocean of buddhas.

Outside, the dance of the consort
    captures the mind
And spreads into every direction:
Inside, one experiences the vast path
    of the union of bliss and void:
Like the flow of a river pursue this practice.

And you who have mastered tantric methods,
Heroes who have accomplished asceticism:
Having totally separated your mind from obscuration,
    preconception and grasping at life as mundane,
Do you not abide in constant joy?

Though practitioners at elementary stages
Are praised by the saints as supreme
For making the smallest meaningful effort,
The same deed, O great ones, would not become you.

By the profound yogas of the secret path,
Such as taking food as ambrosial substances offered
To the dakas and dakinis who reside in the
        channels and energy forces of the body,
One's every action becomes tantric practice.

Having committed yourself to safeguarding the Doctrine,
Wear the armour of mental tenacity
And with the four ways of benefitting the world
Open a hundred doors of universal goodness.

May the sublime, joyous teachings thrive;
May the lineage holders live long;
And may living beings endless as space
Be moved to attain enlightenment.

The colophon: This song on all the principal points of the path combining the Sutras and Tantras was written at the request of the great Chang Kya Rinpoche, a supreme being who accomplished his own noble prayers and aspirations by safeguarding the Buddhadharma in this degenerate age. This work contains nothing not found in the song I wrote for him earlier, but because he persistently asked for another, I wrote it to satisfy his constant requests.

Kelsang gyatso, the seventh Dalai Lama

Lama Tzong-khapa

Foundation for the Preservation of the Mahayana Tradition

The Foundation for the Preservation of the Mahayana Tradition is a worldwide organization dedicated to preserving and communicating the buddhadharma according to the lineage of Lama Tzong-khapa.

Lama Thubten Yeshe and Lama Thubten Zopa Rinpoche gave teachings to their first group of westerners in Nepal, in 1969. This original group has grown to thousands and now year-round teachings are attended by hundreds of students annually, at Kopan, a monastery overlooking the Kathmandu valley.

In 1974 Lama Yeshe and Rinpoche were invited by some of these students to teach in the United States and Australia. Each year since then the lamas have gone on a teaching tour, lasting several months and taking them from the Far East to Europe. Inspired by the dharma and their teachers' dedication to spreading the teachings students have established centres for dharma study and meditational practice in their own countries. There are now eighteen such centres ranging from the residential college and community of sixty-five at Manjushri Institute in England, to Tushita Retreat Centre in the Himalayan foothills of India, to small groups meeting regularly for study and meditation in New Zealand.

Three of the centres have resident geshes (a degree conferred on highly qualified scholars and meditators in the Gelugpa monastic universities of Tibet) who are responsible for the teaching programmes and spiritual life of the communities. Living in most of the centres are a number of western monks and nuns, from among eighty people who have taken lifelong ordination. They play an active role in the community as teachers and counsellors, and participate in the daily schedule of work, meditation and teachings with the lay members of the centre.

The general programme in the centres includes daily teachings by the geshes on all aspects of buddhist meditation and philosophy, as well as short-term meditation courses taught by the geshes and senior ordained and lay students. In addition to traditional dharma the centres are involved in such subjects as art, medicine, yoga, massage, and Tibetan language.

Centres in Australia, England and Italy have begun Geshe Programmes for western students, adapted from the traditional Tibetan monastic system. This unique advanced course of study, available to both men and women, in their own language, will span approximately twelve years, giving students a rigorous buddhist education, leading them to become realized teachers themselves.

Each centre is an environment where, through study, meditation and action, each person can develop wisdom and compassion as a way of life.

The Foundation's headquarters is at Kopan Monastery. This is also the home of the Mount Everest Centre for Buddhist Studies, a monastic school for more than eighty monks, including Tibetans, Sherpas and westerners. These young monks follow an intensive fifteen year course that adheres closely to the Tibetan system. Their studies are preparing them to be future teachers and translators, creating a vital link in the transmission of the buddhadharma to the West.

Another aspect of the Foundation is Publications for Wisdom Culture, established under the directorship of Lama Yeshe as a further means of communicating the dharma to westerners. The long-term goal of Wisdom Culture is translation and publication of the entire buddhist canon. This monumental task is essential if the unbroken tradition of mahayana buddhism is to be preserved.

Nepal
Kopan Monastery, PO Box 817, Kathmandu

India
Tushita Meditation Centre, 5/5 Shanti Nicketan, New Delhi 110021
Tushita Retreat Centre, McLeod Ganj, Dharamsala, H.P.

Australia
Chenrezig Institute, Highlands Road, Eudlo, Queensland 4554
Bodhicitta House, 10 Lomond Terrace, East Brisbane, Queensland 4164
Tara House, 12 Miller Grove, Kew, Melbourne, Victoria 3101

New Zealand
Dorje Chang Institute, Box 2814, Auckland
Dorje Chang Institute, 75 Douglas McLean Avenue, Napier
Dorje Chang Institute, 19a Chelmsford Street, Ngiao, Wellington

England
Manjushri Institute, Conishead Priory, Ulverston, Cumbria LA12 9QQ
Manjushri Institute, 14c Oseney Crescent, London NW5

United States
Vajrapani Institute, Box 295, Santa Monica, California 90406
Vajrapani Institute, Box 82, Boulder Creek, California 95006
Vajrapani Institute, 2964 Shasta Street, Berkeley, California 94708

Italy
Istituto Lama Tsong Khapa, 56040 Pomaia, Pisa

Spain
Nagarjuna Institute, Apartado 971, Ibiza

Holland
Maitreya Institute, M.S. Onderneming, Ouderkerkerdyk, 1096 CS Amsterdam

France
Vajra Yogini Institute, 54 Rue d'Hautpoul, 75019 Paris